Survival in a Down Economy

A Budget Reduction Process for Superintendents

E. E. (Gene) Davis and Jack A. Coffland

Published in partnership with the
American Association of School Administrators

ROWMAN & LITTLEFIELD EDUCATION
A division of
ROWMAN & LITTLEFIELD PUBLISHERS, INC.
Lanham • New York • Toronto • Plymouth, UK

Published in partnership with the American Association of School Administrators

Published by Rowman & Littlefield Education
A division of Rowman & Littlefield Publishers, Inc.
A wholly owned subsidiary of The Rowman & Littlefield Publishing Group, Inc.
4501 Forbes Boulevard, Suite 200, Lanham, Maryland 20706
http://www.rowmaneducation.com

Estover Road, Plymouth PL6 7PY, United Kingdom

British Library Cataloguing in Publication Information Available

Library of Congress Cataloging-in-Publication Data

Davis, E. E., 1938-
  Survival in a down economy : a budget reduction process for superintendents / E. E. (Gene) Davis and Jack A. Coffland.
    p. cm.
  Includes bibliographical references.
  ISBN 978-1-60709-753-2 (cloth : alk. paper) -- ISBN 978-1-60709-754-9 (pbk. : alk. paper) -- ISBN 978-1-60709-755-6 (electronic)
  1. School districts--United States--Administration--Handbooks, manuals, etc. 2. School superintendents--United States--Handbooks. 3. School budgets--United States--Handbooks. 4. Education--United States--Finance--Handbooks. I. Coffland, Jack A. II. Title.
  LB2817.3.D38 2010
  371.2'06--dc22   2010005913

♾™ The paper used in this publication meets the minimum requirements of American National Standard for Information Sciences—Permanence of Paper for Printed Library Materials, ANSI/NISO Z39.48-1992.

Printed in the United States of America

Table of Contents

Acknowledgments

Preparing a manual to describe how to successfully reduce school district budgets during a financial crisis takes time, experience, advice, and patience. First and foremost, the authors appreciate the support, council, and proofreading skills of our wives, Andrea and Cindi. Obviously, without their support, this manual would never have been completed.

Next, we would like to acknowledge the counsel of Dr. Ted Creighton, Dr. Scott Crane, Dr. Ivan Fitzwater, Dr. Thomas Kersten, and Mr. Guy Bellville, who wrote the endorsements and foreword for this manual. Each also spent time reading draft chapters, requesting clarification on specific issues, and preparing final written comments. They are professional colleagues we respect for their candor and support.

Further, the authors would like to thank all of the individuals, too numerous to mention here, who have worked with and/or supervised our professional careers, and for their commitment to excellence and steadfast support when a financial crisis had to be addressed.

In addition, our thanks to Julia Loy, Associate Editor of Production at Rowman and Littlefield, who guided us through the preparation of this manual. Her assistance was precise and thorough.

Finally, we would like to acknowledge the superintendents, fiscal officers, and university executives who are currently involved with leading their institutions through a financial crisis. We are confident you have the leadership skills to weather the current financial storm. We have, in this manual, attempted to offer advice based upon real life experiences that may be helpful to you and those you lead.

Gene Davis and Jack Coffland

Foreword

I am proud and honored to write this Foreword to Davis and Coffland's seminal manual, *Survival in a Down Economy: A Budget Reduction Process for Superintendents.* I am especially thrilled that they have taken the risk to veer from tradition and the status quo and present the profession and its school leaders with strategies and tools designed around actual practice. Sitting superintendents and school board members in the field continue to tell us that what they do in their daily lives as school administrators has little resemblance to their preparation received at the university or state departments of education.

Education leadership has long been criticized by a "disconnect between what is taught in university preparation programs and what practitioners need to be able to do in their schools and districts" (Cambrone-McCabe 1999; English 2008; Murphy 2007; Young, Petersen, and Short 2001). Though much of the reform movement consistently includes the call for closing the gap between theory and practice, the question still remains: Has any significant movement toward this goal occurred?

For some time I have argued for the implementation of a "leadership practice field" for school leaders, both practicing and aspiring. The conceptual notion at work here is that of creating a bridge between the *performance field* (working in the system) and a *practice field* (working on the system). This model is based on the work of Daniel Kim, a colleague of Peter Senge (*The Fifth Discipline*) and cofounder of the MIT Organizational Learning Center. Let me say up front and emphatically, *Survival in a Down Economy: A Budget Reduction Process for Superintendents* is truly the first "leadership practice field" to come along during my thirty years in education. The manual is chocked full of practical examples and illustrations useful to school leaders and boards of education as they face the trying times of financing their education programs for teachers and students.

I can think of no other profession that does not value or provide opportunities for new professionals to practice: in a different kind of space where one can practice and learn. The medical profession has a "practice field," the legal profession has a "practice field," musicians and dancers have a "practice field," the New York Knicks have a "practice field," pilots and astronauts have a "practice field," and on and on. But do we really have a practice field where school superintendents and board members can practice? I argue not; our present preparation and development programs for school superintendents are notoriously weak. The central idea is that a *leadership practice field* provides an environment in which school leaders can experiment with alternative strategies and policies, test assumptions, and practice working through the complex issues of school budgeting in times of crisis. Davis and Coffland have designed such a leadership practice field. And as a former superintendent and now a professor working in university preparation programs, I say: "FINALLY! A manual truly focused on the realities superintendents face and a manual that provides processes to have in place when budget crisis occurs. *Survival in a Down Economy: A Budget Reduction Process for Superintendents* provides the tools and opportunities to practice in all kinds of situations and in all sizes and flavors of school districts (i.e., small, medium, large, rural or urban). I suggest the authors' choice of a *manual* relates to my position here. When I think of a book, I think of something to read. But when I think of a manual, I think of something to mess with, to get my hands on, and to *practice* with.

I stated early on that the authors have dared to veer from tradition in their approach to school budgeting. You will not find the normal "packaged" strategies presented in university preparation programs in this manual. Nor will you find the "packaged" professional development delivered by consultants and state departments of education in this manual. The authors are clear about their purpose and intent: This is not a typical planning manual, designed for normal budgeting with some expected growth each year but a book which discusses budget planning for hard times, especially in times of financial crisis. In reviewing this manuals multitude of practical scenarios and case studies, I tried to think of a budgeting problem that I faced in my years of two superintendencies that Davis and Coffland left out, and I couldn't come up with one. These two experienced school leaders have successfully addressed the "disconnect between what is taught in superintendent preparation programs and what school leaders need to be able to do in their school districts."

Though the authors clearly state the purpose of their manual is to help school superintendents and school boards of small, medium, and large districts address serious financial crisis, I suggest their target audience is far greater that they realize. There are approximately 450 universities who prepare school leaders, especially school superintendents. And we must not neglect the fact that many of those prepared in principal preparation programs move on to superintendent positions bypassing formal superintendent preparation (e.g., California and others). My point is we should realize budgeting in times of crisis applies equally to practicing and aspiring principals who will eventually move into upper-level administrative positions. I also argue that if we wait until superintendents are seated to prepare them to handle the difficult tasks related to school budgeting, it's too late!

My last comment is directed to all those who *aspire* and are *in preparation* to be school leaders: This manual, will prepare you well. I am confident that with the experience you receive in working through these very real case studies and scenarios, you will be ready for the difficult and complex tasks ahead of you. Most importantly, you will be ready to significantly impact teaching and learning in your school.

Theodore B. Creighton
Professor, Educational Leadership & Director of Research & Doctoral Studies, Virginia Tech University
Executive Director, National Council of Professors of Educational Administration (2000-2005)

Basic Assumptions for This Manual on School Budgeting in Times of Crises

This practical manual is written to help school superintendents and school boards address a serious financial crisis, either current or impending, requiring the district to implement major budget reductions. The manual suggests a six-step model to use when facing financial crises. There are assumptions behind both the general model and the recommendations given here; these assumptions are stated here as answers to basic questions that must be addressed when a financial crisis exists.

Major Assumptions of This Manual

Where and when should the recommended budget reduction process be used?

> *Assumption 1: The budget reduction process recommended in this manual is to be used in virtually any size school district that faces a major financial crisis.*

A major financial crisis means the school district will face sizeable budget reductions in (a) the current school year, (b) the upcoming school year, or (c) over the next several years. Such a financial crisis will definitely impact, negatively, the ability of the district to provide a quality educational program for the students it serves.

Who should use the recommended budget reduction process?

> *Assumption 2: Superintendents who believe in a shared decision-making process.*

Without a solid belief in collaborative decision-making processes, superintendents should not attempt to use this budget reduction process. Why? Because a basic principle of the process recommended here is "Those doing the work, the people closest to the work, must be involved in reducing the cost of that work."

Who should *not* use the recommended budget reduction process?

> *Assumption 3: Superintendents who believe all power and authority resides in the hands of the superintendent and the school board.*

Essentially, a "lone ranger" leadership style, coupled with "the school board knows all" attitude, will fail if this budget reduction process is attempted. The process empowers everyone in the budget reduction task; so power must actually be given if everyone is to *stay* involved. Final approving authority rests with the superintendent and school board; but ideas, suggestions, and support rests with the people, everyone, involved in the process.

Notes on the Examples and Illustrations Included in the Text

This manual will provide suggestions, examples, and illustrations of how school districts of difference size faced and reacted to severe financial crises.

Note 1

School Size and the Examples:

Finally, specific examples will be given for districts of different sizes. All "School A" examples are for large districts, "School B" examples for medium sized districts, and "School C" examples for small districts. Brainstorming lists may or may not apply to districts of every size, but such "idea lists" will be given without a school size heading. The lists are provided simply as examples of how district personnel should examine every possibility when considering budget reduction.

These examples come from the author's experiences with schools in different states, during different times, and facing different levels of financial cuts. Therefore, a statement is needed as we begin:

Note 2

Warning for Readers: Our examples are illustrations; the reader must examine each to see if the example is both legal and possible in his or her district.

Presenting past examples of budget reduction situations, or making specific recommendations for budget cuts using real school examples, are both difficult for the authors. There is one major reason: Budgeting processes are different for school districts in different states and for situations in different times. One fact should be obvious to the reader: State restrictions are different. Not all state laws are the same; not all funding formulas are the same; not all funding amounts are the same. Similarly, restrictions on personnel actions are different; they have varied over time and they still vary from state to state. Any personnel example used may have been legal in one state and not legal in that same state today, or an action may be legal in one state and not be legal in your state. The reader must treat examples as examples, not solutions.

The reader should remember that inflation and differences in state funding levels dramatically change school funding amounts over time or between states. This can make a real example from the past unreal in terms of today's dollars, as can dollar examples between states. But the examples are valid in terms of percentages. Cutting 15 percent of a budget presents the same problem for all superintendents, regardless of whether a district receives an allotment of $5,000 per student or $10,000 per student, or whether teacher salaries once averaged $20,000 a year against $50,000 now.

Therefore: The examples and illustrations presented here are for illustration only; the laws, financial formulas, or funding amounts in each reader's state may be dramatically different. The authors' purpose is to illustrate concepts with real examples from real school districts in a variety of states. Readers must consider all examples in terms of the laws and financial practices of their own state. In later chapters this becomes most important; when making specific recommendations for budget cuts, all recommendations must be considered in terms of the laws and regulations of the reader's state.

Section I

Introduction

Chapter One

Budgeting in Times of Fiscal Crisis

Success is uncommon. Therefore not to be enjoyed by the common
man. I'm looking for uncommon people. (Dungy 2009)

Chapter Assumptions: Three basic assumptions must be stated as this manual begins.
1. The reader is currently a superintendent, fiscal officer or school board member in a district facing a severe financial crisis.
2. The reader wishes to become a school administrator prepared to face a severe financial crisis when it (inevitably) occurs.
3. A superintendent, fiscal officer, or school board member who realizes financial crises can be the result of many different economic conditions from local to international. As a result, they may last for different periods of time.

Chapter Objectives: Given the assumptions stated above, there are two objectives for this chapter.
1. State and explain the purpose of this manual.
2. Describe financial realities for public schools when:
   a. Financial uncertainty is the norm;
   b. Schools, as everyone else, face budget reductions.

For School District A: *The Check Will Not Be in the Mail*

A blustery March morning: You're at work as superintendent of the state's largest school district. You know a large portion of the state revenue comes from oil sales; you know oil prices are falling. Newspaper headlines trumpet the state's financial problems daily. Falling oil prices have a direct, negative impact on the state budget. So the drop in oil revenue will seriously, and negatively, impact your budget.

You've already been considering ways to cut next year's budget. Common sense suggested that substantially reduced state revenue would require substantial reductions in your district's budget. Then: your private phone rings; the secretary answers; she buzzes. It's the governor's chief of staff and it is not a social call. You listen, take notes, and then frown. There is no discussion; facts don't change. You thank him for the personal call, and you will help spread the message. You hang up to consider his words and their impact.

Your district's annual budget is $247 million. By March most of this year's budget has already been spent or encumbered. You've just been told $15 million will be held back from this year's fund-

ing; a second holdback this year is probable once the shortfall is fully analyzed. In addition, next year's budget will (a) maintain all cuts from this year, and (b) will require still more reductions.

You examine your notes. In round numbers, a first cut of $15 million, right now! Probably another cut, up to $10 million, this year, and next year's funding reduced an additional $15 to $20 million. If oil revenues continue to decline, even more cuts might be possible next year. In percentage figures, funding cuts are nearing 20 percent of your total budget and the end is not in sight!

And you know one additional fact. Your district is growing. Fast! You enroll over 37,000 students; projections suggest 1,500 new students will enter next year. You will have to teach more students with less money. It will be a lot less money! Your district faces a serious declining revenue situation.

After thinking this situation through, you change your mind. *Your district has a financial crisis.*

The Purpose of the Manual

This manual is written for the "uncommon superintendent." Finding success in a period of financial crisis is definitely uncommon. So the manual is written to help school superintendents in budget planning. It is not the typical planning book, designed for normal budgets with some expected growth each year. The purpose of this manual is to discuss budget planning for hard times, especially times of financial crisis. It is designed for all school administrators who must cut budgets, but it is written especially for those making severe cuts. *It is written for uncommon people facing uncommon problems.*

The manual is not designed to help administrators deal with a 3 percent budget holdback. It can be used for such planning, but budget reductions of that size are not terribly difficult. (They may force tough decisions, but everyone has faced those budget cuts and tough decisions during times of economic downturns.) *The purpose of this manual is to define and present a model for cutting budgets in true crisis times.* The process described in this manual was born and developed when a district was asked to cut 22.3 percent of its budget in two years as enrollment increased. Yet in this district, despite the massive budget cuts, class size did not increase dramatically, few teachers lost their jobs, and the district's employees, along with their unions, actually supported the superintendent and school board throughout the process. And student achievement did increase, new students were incorporated into the district, and employee morale was high. Morale was of vital concern, as the district had gone through a massive strike just a few short years before the budget crisis occurred.

And so, the key questions. How did this all happen? How could a district with a recent strike history come together to solve a major financial crisis, and be proud of their accomplishments?

Financial Crises from Three Decades of Changing Financial Environments

Consider the following three quotes that deal with the funding of public education during the last three decades. It should be apparent that educators have had ample historical examples suggesting that budget cuts and reduced funding are trends that have occurred before and will most likely continue, or even increase, during the next decade.

> Two major trends are apparent in education . . . increasing pressure for school improvement and the reduction of resources for public schools. (Duke 1984)

> The environment for increases in real school revenue per pupil . . . will not be favorable. The most significant problem is likely to be reductions in federal aid to states.

States will respond to decreases in federal aid for social and health programs by trimming increases in state education aid. (Gold 1995)

The holdbacks in the 2008 budget year will be permanent.
Future cuts are also probable.
Tim Hill, Deputy Superintendent, Idaho DOE. (Personal Communication, Dec. 2, 2008)

These three quotes span the last three decades; all paint a negative picture for educational funding. They are included for two reasons. First, financial backing for education has been uncertain for some time. Funding uncertainty is one fact every school superintendent and board member must keep in mind. Severe disruptions in funding patterns are possible at any time. Second, budget reductions, some mild, some severe, have already been mandated several times. Faced with such realities, a prudent superintendent should have *in place* a process to use when budget crises occur.

Beginning in 1983 with *A Nation at Risk*, self-styled critics began voicing fundamental concerns about public education. Those expressing negative viewpoints often felt accuracy was not an important issue; they intended to advance political or social agendas at the expense of public education. (For an example, read *The Manufactured Crisis,* Berliner and Biddle's 1998 response to the content of *A Nation at Risk.*) The school superintendent, however, should see one major fact emerging from the discussion. During the 1980s, it became *popular* to criticize public education and to question its practices, its budgets, and its record. But educational critics and their concerns do not constitute the agenda for this manual. Of greater concern here is one simple fact.

> *All concerns raised, whether right or wrong, have direct and indirect financial implications for public education.*

The issues and concerns expressed, stemming from either thoughtful questions or self-serving opinions, fundamentally impact both (a) the way education is funded and (b) the amount of that funding. School leaders, superintendents and board members, must be prepared to face severe fluctuations in school financing. And both superintendents and board members must realize that funding fluctuations stem from different forces working at different levels in different times. Consider the following:

1. National Economic Trends Affecting Public Education Financing

During the last three decades America faced several periods of recession, some mild, some severe. During those decades governments increased debt, held back funds, or actually cut allocated funds, all negatively impacting school budgets. For example, the national debt increased from approximately $1 trillion to $11 trillion from 1981 through 2008. Increasing debt leads to inflation, and inflation erodes funding, even when dollar amounts remain the same. Allocated dollars simply purchased less. During the same time period, some states incurred similar debt increases. All such debt erodes funding for public education, either in actual dollars or through the erosion of a dollar's purchasing power.

Price fluctuations in natural resources or manufactured goods also impacted the dollars available for education. From fluctuations in oil prices to problems in banking and mortgage services, national economic concerns worked their way down to a school's budget. When that impact suddenly exceeds small holdbacks, a budget crisis can occur.

Everyone is aware of the history of oil price changes and banking problems, but other national trends exist which might cause problems for a district. And it is especially important to consider the budget impact of multiple forces acting at the same time.

School District C:

School District C is located in a silver mining region. During the 1970s, with silver at $6 an ounce, local mines competed well. Then attempts to control the silver market raised the price to record levels. But when sanity returned to the market, the price of silver fell to $3 an ounce and the mines closed. At the same time timber sale dollars, funds given to rural districts housing national forests, were stopped. In some districts, including District C, these dollars were a large part of the total district budget.

Attempts to develop a tourist industry were started, federal superfund dollars were provided to clean up mining areas, and student enrollment dropped. RIFs occurred yearly. Unemployment was high, property tax revenues fell, bond payments were due. Student demographics changed; high achieving students moved out of the district, many students entering the district came with IEPs. Increases in the local levy could not be passed.

In this district, necessary budget cuts would have exceeded 20 percent of the total budget in a short period, if enrollment had remained steady. But revenue fell even further as enrollment dropped from 3,500 students to approximately 1,500 students. In a word, the school district faced a tremendous reduction in revenue from both reduced enrollment and reduced funding on a per student basis.

Clearly, school districts, even as local government units, are not immune to national or international economic fluctuations. District C suffered as two national economic changes impacted the district at the same time. Similarly, the banking and credit crises of 2008 sent shockwaves through the entire national economic system, disrupting home sales, auto sales, and any other type of business requiring credit. As a result, "the economic stimulus packages of 2008 and 2009" have (a) increased the national debt by nearly $2 trillion and (b) disrupted normal revenue streams from which tax dollars for school districts are collected. School district budgets were impacted in the short term by disruptions in tax collections and in the long term by the inflationary impact of huge increases in debt.

2. State Trends Affecting Public Education Financing

National trends usually impact all states, but often in different ways. Some states follow the federal pattern of incurring greater and greater amounts of state debt. In at least one state the debt amount has grown to the point where the governor and state legislatures cannot agree upon a state budget. In this case, as this manual is being written, the final impact upon school districts has not been determined. It seems certain that severe budget cuts will occur. Debt increases inflation even as budget cuts must be made. Such loss of purchasing power, coupled with an actual decrease in funding, will create major budget crises for some school districts.

But other state constitutions require balanced budgets; state debt is not allowed. So, in times of recession, budget holdbacks during the budget year have become common. The impact of holding back or cutting allocated funds is direct and easy to understand: the district simply has fewer dollars. But, as with District C, budget crises occur when funding problems come in bunches. It should be easy to see that combining a first round of holdbacks or budget cuts with a second round of holdbacks and cuts can easily result in major problems. When budget holdbacks are combined with the eroding purchasing power of allocated dollars, districts may suddenly find themselves facing major financial problems.

The combining of cuts is serious. The compounding of problems, a waterfall or cascading effect, can quickly change a "declining revenue situation" into a "budget crisis." Consider the following example of how combined problems hurt a district.

School District B:

School District B is located in a state that must have a balanced budget. Many school districts in the state traditionally use local levies to augment state funding. During a recession, state budget dollars can be held back to assure a balanced state budget. That happened during the prior year. Then the reduced amount became next year's budget base; and as the recession deepened, even more cuts were proposed for the upcoming budget.

School District B has utilized a local levy for years. When the state proposed additional cuts, District B proposed a 25 percent increase in its local levy despite the recession. The increased levy was soundly defeated. The prior or existing levy was presented for a second election and defeated by the voters. When the existing levy was not renewed. District B suddenly faced a loss of those local funds (8.33 percent of the total budget) in addition to the state cuts.

Altogether, District B faced a loss of over 6 percent of state funds and 8.33 percent from their local levy. The reductions forced the district to face budget cuts of 14 percent from one year to the next.

In addition to economic factors, political factors also have an impact upon local school budgets. While voters complain about taxes, it is usually difficult to change the national tax picture. But voters can place referendums onto state ballots. In past years voters placed severe property tax restriction referendums onto ballots; in several states voters passed these initiatives. The approval of property tax restrictions removed a tool used by many districts to augment state funding. Whether property taxes were used to construct new buildings or simply to augment the local school budget, the removal of these dollars caused major damage to many school districts accustomed to such funding. The following example illustrates the measures a desperate superintendent had to take when a state property tax limitation went into effect.

School District A:

State voters approved a 1 percent property tax limitation initiative in a statewide election. While legislators promised increased appropriations for schools, the amounts actually voted were small, ensuring budget cuts for most districts. The expenses of those districts where voters historically approved supplemental levies were simply not covered. Budget cuts in these districts were large. So, despite planned cuts and a small increase in the state allocations, revenues did not match expenses.

Early one January morning in District A an experienced first grade teacher was surprised to see the superintendent waiting in her classroom. Years before she had been hired during the school year; on that January morning she had reached exactly thirty years of service. The superintendent was there to make a request.

If she were to officially retire, he would rehire her for the remainder of the school year at a beginning teacher's salary. Her state retirement, coupled with that salary, would give her a slight pay increase for the remainder of the school year. And the district would save approximately $15,000 in salary and benefits! For that desperate superintendent, $15,000 was the largest budget saving he could obtain that day; therefore, meeting the teacher was the first task on his calendar that January morning.

The program for addressing budget cuts presented in this manual is especially useful when budget problems cascade. Multiple factors, including economic, political, or financial, occurring at the same time created true financial emergencies requiring a thorough program of planning for budget cuts.

3. *Local Economic Trends Impacting School Financing*

Superintendents and school boards know some portion of school funding comes from local tax sources. Therefore, local economic factors have major impacts upon school budgets and school financing. The closing of a factory, a drop in the price of a farm commodity, or even the failure of a bond or operations levy can have major negative impacts on the local school district budget.

School District C:

School District C enrolled approximately 2,000 students and seemed to be growing due to its "bedroom community" location near a larger city. A bond election was passed to build a new high school; debt payments were a new, large factor in the district's budget. As the new building was completed, however, a factory located in the town closed. Property tax revenues fell, student enrollment dropped slightly, and payments on the building levy began, all at the same time. The budget crisis was severe; cuts in the realm of 18 percent were required.

Such local changes in school funding occur for different reasons; many are completely unrelated to state and national economic conditions. But when they occur, the impact upon a local school's budget can be quite severe. But the worst problems emerge when budget problems occur in clusters. For School District C the building levy and the factory closing occurred together and presented the district with a budget problem demanding attention. A simple 5 percent across the board cut in every budget area would not begin to address the financial emergency. School officials needed a comprehensive plan to address budget reduction; "across the board" cuts of this magnitude were not possible.

District C actually tried moving to a four-day school week as a short-term solution to the problem. Again, there are always reasons against using a one step solution to budget problems, reasons that will vary from one district to another. But in District C the percentage of latchkey children was small; the four-day week did not impact the majority of parents. But in many districts a four-day week solution would impact working parents so severely that such a solution would cause more problems than it solved. Parents have become used to the school week matching their work week. In districts with large percentages of latchkey children the district performs a major child-care service to working parents; such a need could make this one-step solution to a budget crisis unusable.

But financial problems in individual districts can stem from any number of causes; regardless of the cause, the budget impact can be severe. Consider the following example.

School District B:

A national corporation selected a regional airport in District B as a location for its freight hub. After years of service, a recession forced the corporation to drop freight operations. Employees of the freight service owned many homes, and were employees of the company. With the closure of the freight hub, jobs left, people moved, and the district lost students. Even if a family did not move, one or more of the adults lost their jobs. Property tax collections decreased as tax valuations were lowered; local business revenues decreased. Even tax collections were reduced when dismissed workers could not pay the taxes. In simple terms, local employment problems caused a severe budget crisis for the district.

The case examples generate one conclusion. A financial crisis can occur in any district at any time based upon national economic trends, state financial concerns, or completely local events. The possibility of fiscal emergencies should suggest one idea to every school superintendent or every school board: *A district should be prepared with a plan or set of procedures to face a budget crisis.* Simple across the board cuts cannot be used to solve such major budget shortfalls. "Business as usual" should not and cannot continue when major portions of the district's revenue stream disappear in a short period of time.

Summary

Therefore, to help superintendents and school boards face uncertain fiscal environment, this manual is written to provide leaders with a proven, effective, and systematic budget assessment process to use in addressing uncertain fiscal situations. If fiscal environments provide new dollars, the budget assessment process should help superintendents spend new dollars (a) in support of and (b) in alignment with documented school district goals.

But if uncertain fiscal environments provide fewer dollars, the process provides guidelines for budget reductions. It helps guide the superintendent and school board in adjusting the budget to meet needed cuts. But, most importantly, if major, catastrophic budget reductions are necessary, then the process will provide school boards and superintendents with planning documents (already in place) and a budgeting process to guide the district through the difficult times. The process described in this manual should help school leaders deal with all types of financial concerns.

Two points should be emphasized. (1) This manual is not written to predict doom. (2) Nor is it written to criticize the way money is presently being spent by school districts. The purpose of the manual is singular. *Any wise school superintendent and every far-sighted school board should have plans in place to handle all financial conditions that might occur.* It is important to emphasize the concept of "any" type of financial condition that might occur.

Most educators are prepared for financial "good" times. Textbooks, college courses, and in-service workshops abound for budgeting processes during times when money supplies are adequate or expanding. But very little is written on planning and budgeting for "bad" times. The superintendent facing a budget downturn will find few workshops, consultants, or other such assistance available. The unfortunate school board and superintendent facing a major budget-cutting task will usually work alone when the crisis occurs. People handle budget increases better than budget decreases! Assistance abounds for superintendents with new money to spend; a superintendent recommending budget cuts stands alone.

The primary purpose of the budget assessment process recommended in this manual is to assist school districts facing budget cuts. It should be obvious that good budget planning never hurts, regardless of the times. But good budget planning is essential when a district faces deep cuts. So all examples and illustrations given in the manual will describe budget reduction situations.

The process has been used several times, even in districts facing catastrophic budget reductions. It has been used in different geographical regions, in both urban and rural school districts. It has been used in districts where a wide range of employee bargaining and non-bargaining groups were involved. It has been used in a district facing cuts in excess of $52 million over a two-year period.

But dollar amounts don't always tell the entire story. Using percentages, the process was used in a district forced to reduce its budget 10 percent in one year and nearly 25 percent over two years. In a worst-case scenario, one district used the process when it was forced to make an 18 percent budget cut *during the last quarter* of the school budget year.

Using the budget analysis and reduction process recommended in this manual, every school district achieved its budget-cutting goal. But much more importantly, in every school district where the process had to be used, the budget reduction was made "successfully," where success is defined as:
1. Achieving a balanced school district budget.
2. Arriving at the reduced budget without acrimony, either within the district or the community.

3. Providing budget recommendations for school board approval with little or no modification.
4. Serving to bind school and community into a renewed partnership using fewer resources.
5. Creating budget reduction recommendations having the lowest possible impact upon the district's classrooms.

Process Expectations

There are several reasons for using a process approach while planning and making budget reductions. They include:

1. The process should yield a variety of suggestions for reducing the budget.
2. The budget analysis and reduction process should provide a clearly defined system for evaluating all budget reduction suggestions.
3. The budget reduction process should help the district focus on sustaining and/or improving the instructional program.
4. The budget reduction process is based upon a consensus decision making strategy to promote unity during difficult times.
5. The budget reduction process should provide guidelines for allocating any increase in funding, when and if the district is so fortunate.

What is this budget analysis process? What are the details? How can it be put into place in a district? When should it be put into place? This manual will present and address these questions.

References

Biddle, Bruce and David Berliner (1998). *The Manufactured Crisis.* Reading, MA: Addison Wesley Publishing Company.

Duke, Daniel L. (1984). *Decision Making in an Era of Fiscal Instability.* Bloomington, IN: p. 7. Phi Delta Kappa Fastback. PDK Educational Foundation.

Dungy, Tony with Nathan Whitaker (2009). *Uncommon: Finding Your Path to Significance.* Carol Stream, IL: Tyndale House of Publishers, Inc.

Gold, Steven D. (1995). *The Outlook for School Revenue in the Next Five Years.* Consortium for Policy Education and Research in Education, Report #34.

Chapter Two

The Budget Reduction Process: An Overview

Make no little plans; they have no magic to stir men's
blood . . . make big plans, aim high in hope and work. (Burnham 2009)

Chapter Assumptions: Four basic assumptions serve as the foundation for this chapter.
1. Using a planned budget reduction system will give everyone a role in the process, from making suggestions to evaluating ideas to implementing the final budget.
2. Incorporating a budget reduction process, one open to all interested parties, will enable the district to consider all suggestions in a fair and impartial manner.
3. The budget reduction process will enable ideas to be debated at the beginning of the process, not at the approval stage.
4. The budget reduction process will require that all suggestions go through the same review process, thus guaranteeing all ideas a complete, impartial review.

Chapter Objectives: Given the assumptions stated above, the objectives for this chapter are:
1. Describe the rationale for the budget reduction process.
2. Describe the six components of the budget reduction process.

The Rationale for the Budget Reduction Process

One thing should be perfectly clear to those who have accessed this manual: A financial catastrophe or loss of revenue for school operations is as much of a school district crisis as an employee strike, a natural disaster, or an organizational scandal. The budget reduction process described in this chapter is founded on basic planning techniques and is designed to avoid reactionary decisions in such times of crisis. Leading a school district during a crisis, in this instance financial uncertainty, is much different than conducting business as usual. Kotter (1996), in his book *Leading Change*, states:

Conducting business as usual is very different if the building seems to be on fire. But in an increasingly fast world, waiting for a fire to break out is a dubious strategy. And, in addition to catching people's attention, a sudden fire can cause a lot of damage. p. 45

School districts are encountering the same rapid change as businesses and the leadership of a district needs to be as attuned to this change as any business executive. The impact of the No Child Left Behind Act (NCLB), the increase in the number and type of charter schools, on-line courses and/or schools, a wide variety of programs available for those who choose not to attend any type of school, court decisions effecting the delivery of Special Education services, the increase of students who require second language instruction, and the increase in the social services that districts are required to provide, all of these should be sufficient evidence of the changing environment for school district leaders. Coupled with the onslaught of state, national and global events that impact available revenue for schools simply confirms the need for district leaders to be prepared for financial uncertainties. This manual provides the basis for that preparation.

The budget reduction planning process described in this manual is designed to serve as the foundation for addressing school district financial uncertainties. The process was born out of necessity when one of the authors was required to deal with a major loss of revenue for a school district during a school year, not once, but twice; and facing additional cuts between school years in the same district. The district had eight bargaining groups, all of which unanimously supported the process. Further, the school board supported the process and with one small exception approved all of the recommended budget cuts. The process was further tested and refined when the same individual dealt with two more instances of financial uncertainty in another district in another state. The budget reduction process was successful in all instances. As a result the authors decided to share this process with other administrators in the desire to increase the success factor in school districts facing financial uncertainty.

This process should enable district superintendents and school board members to adapt, change, and/or modify the way budgets are prepared and analyzed during times of a financial crisis. The process has six steps. Each of the steps will be briefly presented in this chapter in order for the reader to see the total process.

A brief note is necessary prior to beginning the description of the six steps. Most economic downturns or major revenue losses do not occur in the dead of the night. The exception is a natural disaster, such as a fire, earthquake, structural collapse of a school building, or other such unanticipated events. Most economic downturns can be projected prior to the occurrence; districts should prepare for or at least be preparing for fiscal problems. But the degree of the downturn may not be predictable.

Budget Reduction Process: An Overview

A chart outlining the six steps is provided to indicate each of the steps in the process. It is critical the administrator and board members view this process in totality. Each step builds on the previous step. To begin this process other than at the beginning could possibly result in confusion and potential disruption of the total budget reduction process in a district. Large districts, those with a variety of departments and personnel, will need to emphasize each part of the process. The need for communication across all levels of the organization will require precise application of all steps in order to ensure consistency. The intensity level with the process will be greater in large school districts. Testimony provided by superintendents in medium to small districts indicates intensity can be reduced through direct communication between those responsible for district operations. In smaller districts superintendents speak directly with department heads and building principals; they do not communicate through subordinates. In small or medium size districts, then, some elements of the process may be modified and/or integrated.

Budget Reduction Process Steps

Step 1	Situational Analysis
Step 2	Establishing the Strategic Direction
Step 3	Idea Generation Stage
Step 4	Idea Analysis Process
Step 5	Staff/Community Evaluation
Step 6	School Board Review and Actions

Step 1: Situational Analysis: This beginning step has important considerations as shown below:

Budget Analysis
- Projected/Anticipated Fund Balance
- Continuation Level Budget
- Projected Budget Situation
- Assumptions and Guiding Principles

Needs Analysis
- Enrollment Projections
- Capital Improvement and Its Effect on Operations and Maintenance
- Budget Contingencies

What Is and Is Not Working
- Existing Programs and Services
- Planned Programs and Services

Example Solutions
- Alternatives: External Revenue Sources
- Alternatives: Internal Revenue Sources
- Budget Reduction Sources

Communication Plan
- Planning the Information Exchanges

The need to create a budget reduction process begins with the district superintendent. The superintendent and school board should implement the steps of the process as school board policy long before any budget reduction situation actually arises. Through this process, the recommended steps are part of board policy and are available to the superintendent and school board when needed.

The budget reduction process begins when the superintendent, as the head of the district, determines that a problem exists. A crisis level problem stems from one key fact: *The continuation level budget for next year and the projected revenue situation for next year are not even close to being aligned.* In other words, a major discrepancy exists between the present budget and the anticipated revenue for next year. But the absolute worst of conditions occurs when a major discrepancy exists between existing revenue and completing the *current* year's budget. The superintendent's staff may assist in making this determination, but in the end, the process begins when the person at the top says, "We have a problem!" and accepts ownership of the problem.

The superintendent must create an overall summary of the situation. That summary must identify the needs for next year, the fact that a shortfall is forecast, and outline some possible solutions. Is the budget shortfall relatively small and solvable by the district's administrative team? Or is it large, requiring major cuts across the entire school district? (The process recommended here, obviously, is designed for the second scenario.) Finally, the superintendent should outline the communication plan that will be used throughout the process. The problem, the general recommendations, and the communication plan must then be shared with the school board. When everyone at the top is convinced that a problem exists, it is time to bring others in to implement the system process recommended here.

Considerable attention must be paid to the actual financial details during the projection of an actual or anticipated revenue reduction. Considerable scrutiny of enrollment figures, expenditure patterns, actual revenue anticipated, required new expenditures, potential revenue sources, and the local economy are critical if accurate information is to be available for planning as a result of this analysis. The worst situation is for the school board and community to find out at a later date that either too large a reduction was anticipated or another source of funds had not been identified. The credibility of the entire process hinges on an accurate beginning analysis.

A myriad of immediate budget reduction options could be available to the district leadership team, depending on state law or board policy. For instance, some states do not permit local districts to cut salaries from one year to the next. Asking leadership team members to reduce salaries might be impossible. However, if salary reductions are possible, the district leadership team might reduce their salaries by a specific dollar amount or a percentage. A leader leads by words and examples; such a voluntary pay cut would definitely make the point that a financial situation is, and will continue to be, serious. A case example explains this point more specifically.

School District A: Leadership Personnel Voluntary Reductions

The superintendent of a large city district was faced with a 20 percent or $42 million reduction in revenue from one year to the next. In addition, the district enrollment projections indicated an additional 1,500 new students would enroll for the next year. The district employed over 7,000 people; of these, only 129 were not represented by a bargaining group.

As a first step, the superintendent decided to reduce his salary by 5 percent, and asked the 129 non-bargaining employees to take a 3 percent reduction in salary. He examined the central office budget, the school board's salaries and expenses, and all travel expenses for district administrators. Cuts in all of these areas were recommended.

As a result, when the superintendent announced the district was facing a financial crisis, he was also able to announce recommendations for cutting $4 million from the budget in administrative salaries, travel, and operation costs. This had a dramatic, positive impact on the eight bargaining groups. Each group decided to either freeze their salaries at current levels or take a percent reduction. The key point is that leaders are the exemplars of the behavior they expect others to demonstrate. This is particularly important in a time of crisis.

Once sufficient data has been collected to substantiate the decision that a financial crisis exists, the superintendent should make the first budget reduction effort. That is the point of the "leading by example" in the school district example provided above. It is important to show that everyone will be making sacrifices, including the central office. When the crisis has been identified and a first cut has been identified for presentation to all stakeholders, then it is time for the superintendent and his/her staff to move on to Step 2 in the budget reduction process.

Step 2: Establishing Strategic Direction: Major considerations at this step of the process include:
> **Basic Definitions**
>> Base Quality Education
>> Essential Support Services
> **Establish Goals**
>> Mission Priorities

       Key Result Areas
Develop Analysis System
       Descriptor Codes to Document/Analyze Proposals
       System for Categorizing Proposed Reductions
Establish Targets
       Size of Reductions Needed From Budget Analysis
       General Reduction Goals By Departments/Schools

Step 2 begins with an analysis of both "base quality education" and "essential support services," using a well defined and published criteria. It is vital to determine what the school district can and cannot do without. Great care must be exhibited in this area; for example, the district does need classrooms, but it may not need a carpentry shop; a building may need a daytime janitor, but nighttime cleaning might be contracted out; a classroom needs a teacher, but it may not need a textbook for every child in every subject. Both the base quality program and the essential support services need to justify their expenditures. For the purpose of this manual, "base quality education" is defined as follows:

> Base quality education is the educational program, with its components, required by state law and the state board of education. It may also include those elements that are outlined in any accreditation association to which the district belongs. Finally, it also includes any program or service(s) the local community values so highly that the district cannot discontinue said program or service.

The base, once established, helps direct attention to the major mission of the district and to the areas where key savings may be expected. The coding system described helps people quickly examine proposed savings; the categorizing system helps those who must make the ultimate decision to understand the repercussions of their decision(s). And finally, out of the development process must come a targeted goal for every division, department, office, and school. The key point is that the district is responsible for providing students a "basic education," whatever level of funding is available. Each department, each building principal, or each support service director must define what will be his or her "bottom line." The district must define, in writing, its "base quality" program. Two essential questions must be (a) previously answered in a district strategic plan, or (b) determined at this stage.
1. What constitutes the "base quality education level" that the district is unwilling to go below?
2. What are the "essential support services" required to deliver a quality education program?

Base quality education is what must be protected in times of budget cuts. *Extras* do not have to be protected, regardless of where they are found. Consider the following examples for electives courses.

School Districts B: Options for Reducing Personnel Costs
    Secondary schools must offer core subject classes to all students. In the NCLB era they must offer special sections to assist students not meeting state standards and/or graduation requirements. But in troubled times, the number, type, and size of elective courses can be regulated. There are several ways to do this.
    High School X, District B: While considering its base quality education, reducing elective secondary classes was considered. The school set enrollment minimum standards for all elective courses. This allowed District B to offer six fewer courses; either a retirement or RIF action would be possible without replacing a teacher. The number of teachers needed was reduced in the school because the number of courses or sections offered would be reduced.

For small and medium size districts, cutting electives may mean setting minimum class size requirements or simply eliminating electives. Large districts have more possibilities.

School District A: Options for Reducing Personnel Costs

High School Y: District A: A large district examined all elective and small enrollment courses in all of its secondary schools. The unique, special interest electives and the small enrollment electives were real possibilities for budget reductions. In that large school district, several high schools were offering one section of Russian each. It was determined that the district could not continue to offer such small enrollment electives in every school, however desirable it might be.

They decided to offer Russian in one high school, thus combining several small class sections into one class. The students were allowed to select either a curriculum transfer to the high school offering the class, or they were allowed to provide their own transportation to attend the class. The net effect was six small sections of the foreign language class were eliminated; this resulted in a personnel reduction of one teacher, both salary and benefits.

The example given above brings home the need to build a relationship with all bargaining units if their contracts are impacted. If teachers made the recommendations given in the above example (by including them on a committee considering the reductions), the chances of (a) actually making the cuts and (b) having teacher support at a board meeting, are considerable. If bargaining group members are not involved in the entire process, then it is highly likely that recommended budget cuts will be opposed by that bargaining unit.

For budget reductions in the service area, consider the following example of redefining levels of direct or indirect support services.

School District A, B, or C: Reducing Custodial Service Costs

Two different possibilities exist for assigning custodial services. First, custodians can be asked to clean a greater area (more square footage.) This might be a bargaining group contract issue or a school board policy. But if custodians were required to clean a larger area, personnel savings might be achieved. Given that such employees often have a higher turnover rate, this option might provide cost savings without requiring a RIF action. Similar "formula driven savings" might be found when redefining responsibilities for both direct and indirect instructional support services. Such positions might include library aides, special education aides, tutors, secretaries, or bookkeepers.

While in this process of defining (or possibility of *redefining* support services), budget reduction opportunities may emerge. The key point in this possible redefining of support services is for the ideas to come from those who work in each support service area. Personnel in each area should be encouraged to find possible reductions that would not require the elimination of personnel. They should be informed that reductions will be needed; creativity in providing ideas in such areas as changing work schedules, weekly hours, job responsibilities or pay scales could result in saving jobs. A straight forward approach to the issue of potential reductions is essential. Employees should be aware that district administration could propose budgets cuts, but prefer to have suggestions from the actual employees.

As an example for question one on page 15, restating or redefining the base level requirements for administrative services are addressed in the following example.

School Districts A, B, and C: Reducing Administrative Costs

Whenever district personnel retire or resign, reorganization should be a consideration in the budget reduction process. An early retirement or the elimination of a district level position would help reduce expenditures for district wide services. Eliminating a position does mean another administrator must assume new responsibilities. Examples include:

(a) In a small district with a superintendent, secondary principal and elementary principal, one superintendent assumed the role of elementary principal to eliminate that position from the budget. (His assumption: The activity supervision load of a secondary principal would make that role more difficult for the superintendent to assume.) Combining two administrative jobs would reduce costs in a small district by a considerable amount.

(b) Medium and large districts should consider reorganization when a possibility occurs, through either an ERIP or a resignation. At these times a reduction can occur without any "reduction in force" (RIF) action. The operating principle for the reorganization is simple: One administrator, with a broad range of responsibilities, is more cost effective than several administrators with limited ranges of supervision.

The defining of base level administrative and/or support services should be part of any strategic plan adopted by the district. If they are not already available, staff time must be allocated to clearly define them. While some may not see the importance of these efforts, they need only be reminded that district patrons and staff will be raising questions about recommended reductions and comparing all suggestions. Comparisons between cuts, and comparison of the size of cuts, can only be made if clear, rational, and defensible answers are provided. Experience with the budget reduction process clearly indicates definable standards need to be (a) determined and (b) available for those working on creating and or reviewing suggested budget cuts.

How are such "base quality education standards" determined? The educational standards for base quality can be identified and/or determined by reviewing state requirements, accrediting association standards, federal mandates, and the research supporting quality instruction. They cover such things as safety, staff, instruction and program standards. Local decisions will be needed regarding the *level* of support for the standards that the district can afford to sustain. Standards from accrediting associations typically define minimum, acceptable, and exceptional levels of service. Can the district now afford only the minimum standard? In other areas, such as safety standards and building capacity, standards cannot be modified. In these areas a careful review is needed to assure all legal minimums are met.

Essential support service standards, those covering issues outside the direct delivery of instruction, can usually be found from business or government guidelines. Examples would include standards for computer replacement or repair, custodial services, building maintenance, employee supervision, and heating or safety standards. Some standards are available from education related groups, such as architects, school bus transportation organizations, and other such associations.

A careful search of available references and closely working with the business community in your area can be of great assistance. A review of community expectations is helpful, particularly if industry standards are not as high as the community expects. One way to summarize the base quality program is to cite that:

• Standards are required by established state law, local ordinance, or state school board rule;
• Standards are referenced in professional publications as being highly desirable;
• No established standard is available, although a set performance level is highly desirable; or
• No required standard is available or appropriate.

Above all else, it is imperative to make reduction decisions based on predetermined criteria, standards, or laws. Anything short of using this approach could result in chaos.

Step 3: Idea Generation Stage: Major considerations for this step include the following:
      Board Policy and Administrative Regulation Review
          Do our policies and regulations have financial implications?
          If so, which policies and/or regulations might be changed?
      Staff and Citizen Idea Input
          Create a "Cost-Busters" program
          Consider possible service elimination
          Possible service restructuring or reductions
      Stakeholder Survey for Reactions
          Which programs are seen as essential for the community?
          Which programs are not?

Once a budget problem is identified and the budget reduction process has begun, everyone begins generating ideas on how to find/create cost savings or revenue enhancements. The school board should examine policies and the administrations should examine existing regulations; these often have financial implications. Accreditation requirements, state department regulations, or legal decisions may need to be collected, analyzed, and reviewed in order to complete this task. On the other hand, a janitor may suggest a less expensive brand of cleaner. No idea should be overlooked, and ideas can come from many different sources. At the state level, an early retirement incentive might exist; if so, it should be used. The district might add an incentive program of its own. Consider:

> **School Districts A, B, and C: State Early Retirement Incentives**
> Many states and school districts have early retirement incentives programs (ERIP). Obviously, those states that have such programs should be encouraging them, especially during a financial crisis. And a school district should be encouraging teachers to examine such programs. It is penny rich and pound foolish to drop such programs in such "hard times" as the nation is currently experiencing.

> **School Districts A, B, and C: Create District Early Retirement Incentives**
> If a state has no ERIP program, it might be worthwhile to consider a district ERIP emergency plan for a specific period of time. A local ERIP could work wonders for the district in two ways. First, an early retirement might reduce the district's costs by the entire salary/benefit package of the retiring person, *if the position does not need to be refilled.* Second, even if the retiring individual must be replaced, the difference between a high level salary and a beginner's salary/benefit package should be significant. In either situation, creating the district's own ERIP with local funds should allow the district to achieve a significant budget reduction.

The board should also define who might suggest cost savings or revenue enhancements. *Everyone* is the recommended answer. Regardless of what a budget reduction idea entails, it is not important to consider who suggested it. Take ideas from wherever they come. But it is important to have involved stakeholders examine the impact of each and every suggestion.

For example, anyone might suggest cutting junior high school competitive athletic programs. But it is important to survey coaches, teachers, players, and parents to see the impact of a suggestion; it is also important to test the idea back against the base quality education definition. In this phase it should be obvious why defining the "base instructional quality" and "essential support services" are part of the strategic planning process. Knowing the bottom line of program options and support service requirements is critical. All proposed savings should be measured against this bottom line.

The "Cost Busters" program is particularly critical in Step 3. A process should be defined that clearly outlines how each reduction suggestion will be analyzed. A recognition program should also be established for those individuals who suggest a budget reduction that is approved. The recognition program need not be expensive. A certificate and a school board thank you is usually sufficient. However, any recognition program should announce the successful recommendation to all school personnel and support staff. This will reinforce the importance of asking each person for any suggestions they might have. The complete Cost Busters program will be described in a later chapter.

Step 4: Idea Analysis Process: This step has four components:
    Creation of All Data on Proposed Cost Reductions or Revenue Enhancements
    Determination of Reduction Evaluation Criteria
    Multi-Level Implement Reduction Evaluation Criteria
    Prepare Reductions for Advisory Committee Analysis and Recommendation

Determining all possible eligible reductions is the focus of Step 4. Data should be prepared on each proposal, showing its cost savings and/or revenue enhancements, along with any predicted impacts upon the base quality program or essential support services. Then, a predetermined criteria for evaluating each possible reduction places everyone on equal footing and substantially enhances communication. A multi-level evaluation process should be used, one that guarantees opportunities for input from each school or district department to comment on the proposals. Finally, this step enables the superintendent to guide major reductions away from direct instruction if at all possible.

Effective representation of proposed reductions requires a coding system that can be easily read and digested by employees and patrons alike. Charts that reflect the codes and the actual impact of proposed reductions need to be prepared by the finance department to assure accuracy of such items as dollar amounts or staffing ratios. Once prepared, the superintendent and the advisory committee receive the information with ample time to review, make inquiries for clarification, and become thoroughly knowledgeable about the information. This basic information set should be provided to everyone *prior* to discussing the implications and acceptance of the proposed budget cuts.

Step 5: Staff Community Evaluation: This step has two major components.
    Consensus Decision-Making Ground Rules
    Determine Final Recommendations
        Identifying pre-consensus considerations
        Presenting recommended reductions
        Resolving concerns
        Identifying options if consensus ss not reached

Structuring the decision making process with guidelines identified up front, accompanied by focused involvement on a specific set of issues, can produce exceptional results. Given that all participants in this step have been key players in Steps 1 through 4, the knowledge level and commitment should be very high. The goal of this step is to develop consensus on reductions that can be supported by all stakeholders when presented to the school board.

The tradition bound individual or group can be a major obstacle to reaching consensus on recommendations. However, omitting a broad spectrum of stakeholders may close communication channels, leave good suggestions unmade, and ignore options that should be considered. Omitting some "tradition bound" group of stakeholders will also ensure that a specific (and vocal) group of people has not been involved in the process. They have not debated other possible cuts, compared the amounts, and seen the ramifications of making versus not making a specific cut. If a group is left out of the discussions, and they are opposed to a specific proposed budget cut or some general area of budget cuts, they *will* come to the final board meeting to oppose all suggestions.

Step 6: School Board Review and Actions: This final step has three elements.
    Presentation Format
    Decision-Making Guidelines
    Communication with the Public and the Media

Embarking on a consensus decision-making process for budget reduction is definitely a different way of doing business. The school board must concur in this approach and respect the results. Given the substantial advance work done by the superintendent, staff, and stakeholders, there should be no surprises for the board. Certainly the board should hold official public hearings on the recommended cuts; but it is critical that all suggested cuts made by those not committed to and involved in the original process must be subject to the same criteria and guidelines that were used to evaluate all original budget reduction suggestions.

The media can help assure that everyone sticks to the process. Providing media representatives with information during the process help publicize and obtain (a) adequate understanding of the recommendations and (b) accurate reporting along the way. Providing copies of the recommended reductions in public libraries, at each school office, and to all civic organizations further keeps the process open. Finally, a "budget hotline" should be set up for those who wish to comment, propose alternatives, or ask questions for clarification.

Each of the steps mentioned here will be outlined in detail in a specific chapter. But first, several other general considerations must be presented, and specific points about leadership and communication should be made and discussed.

References

Burnham, Daniel. Retrieved November 3, 2009, www.desktop-quotes.com/words of wisdom.

Kotter, John (1996). *Leading Change.* Boston, MA: Harvard Business School Press.

Chapter Three

Who Should Use This Process?

The first responsibility of a leader is to define reality.
(DePree 2009)

Chapter Assumptions: Three basic assumptions serve as the foundation for this chapter.
1. The budget reduction process is designed for use by superintendents of small, medium or large districts in any state.
2. The process does not require specialized staff to be implemented.
3. The process is especially useful in times of financial crisis.

Chapter Objectives: This chapter will address the objectives that follow.
1. Provide a historical example of how and why the process was developed.
2. State and explain procedures for using the process in a school district.
3. Provide an example of how a medium sized school district used the process.

Budget Reduction Process: A History

The budget reduction process described in this manual was first developed in a large school district, enrolling approximately 37,000 students, during a period of financial uncertainty in the mid-1980s. To be specific, the district was asked to cut nearly $15 million from its existing budget with only three months left in that budget year. Additional cuts followed rapidly. Between April of one school year and November of the next school year, the district was forced to cut $52 million from a budget of $247 million. This computes to a 21 percent budget cut, but it did not come that way to the district. The district was first asked to cut $15 million, and then another $8 million in the last ninety days of a budget year. Additional cuts of $17 million and $12 million were made in the budget for the next school year.

The district was located in an oil state, and the price of oil fell from a high of $34.10 a barrel back to a low of under $13.43 a barrel over several years. It was the speed of the decline after 1985 that caused a major shortfall in expected revenue for the state. The exact prices are shown in chart 1.

Chart 1
Oil Price Declines
1981 through 1987

Year	Oil Price Per Barrel	Percent of 1981 Prices	Percent Drop from 1981
1981	$34.10	na	na
1982	$30.28	88.8%	11.2%
1983	$28.04	82.2%	17.8%
1984	$26.77	78.5%	21.5%
1985	$26.27	77.0%	23.0%
1986	$21.52	63.1%	36.9%
1987	$13.43	39.4%	60.6%

Source: Alaska Dept. of Revenue/Tax Division/Oil Prices

The problems faced by the superintendent were obvious. First, deep cuts in the budget were ordered well into a school year. Cutting $15 million from a budget at the beginning of the school year would be a problem; cutting that many dollars in the final four months of a budget year, after the majority of the year's budget had already been spent and/or encumbered, was much more difficult. This immediately created a budget crisis for the district. The second cut of $8 million that came during the same budget year simply compounded the crisis.

But as the price of oil continued to fall, it was obvious that additional cuts were coming. The state's revenue expectations were lower than predicted, and the continued fall in oil prices led to ever-lowering expectations for the upcoming year. Most importantly from a budget projection point of view, the bottom was not in sight. How far the state's revenues were going to fall could not even be predicted when the budget crisis was first identified.

The superintendent correctly saw he was in a budget crisis situation. A simple across the board holdback was not a possible solution, especially when the first major holdback, coming at the end of the year, was already a 6 percent cut. That first cut came with a message that another cut might be needed before the end of that same budget year. This would qualify as a severe budget crisis for any school district. A simple across the board cut, coming late in the year, would not solve the problem. Since additional cuts were looming, the superintendent needed a process that would identify any additional budget cuts.

The Problem and Possible Solutions

The superintendent identified a budget crisis; it was already deep and it was getting deeper daily. The bottom was not yet in sight. Projected budget cuts were going much deeper than any simple plan would solve. The district had to change the way business was done at a fundamental level. In addition, the student population was still growing, and continued to grow during the entire budget crisis. The superintendent was faced with choosing between two different scenarios.

First, he could order budget cuts "across the board" for everyone, in every building, every department, and every program. He immediately perceived this would cause a large number of problems. The cuts were going to be so deep that "across the board" cuts would mean (a) teachers would be fired, (b) class size would increase dramatically, (c) departments might be unable to do their job, and (d) individual programs might be cut so deeply that sustaining any portion of the program would be useless.

But what would be the basis for determining the specific cuts. How would the district identify programs that stayed versus those that were cut? Maintenance savings could not be obtained by closing buildings; the district was still increasing in student body count. More students would mean purchasing more school busses and hiring more drivers; across the board cuts would mean exactly the opposite. More students would mean more classrooms and more teachers, or larger classes and fewer teachers.

Finally, and most importantly, any school superintendent dictating budget cuts of that magnitude from the central office would create a firestorm within the district. All cuts ordered from above would be contested. School board meetings would have to be held in an auditorium in order to hold the parents, bargaining group members, and program staff desiring to argue against virtually every cut. Budget reductions of such a magnitude would be extremely divisive. Meetings would be lengthy; blood would be on the floor after every single school board meeting.

One other point should be obvious. A superintendent dictating cuts from the central office, or ordering all cuts on an "across the board" basis, would be literally walking the plank. He or she would be standing alone at the end of the plank while critics already had a saw cut extending half way through the plank. He or she would only be following orders, but the superintendent proposing all changes would be the single recipient for everyone's anger on every recommended budget cut. He or she would be the focal point for that anger, from every parent, employee, bargaining group, and taxpayer. To use a different metaphor, the superintendent would only be the messenger of the bad news, but public reaction would focus on shooting the messenger!

A Process Was Born

The superintendent clearly saw the total picture. The district faced budget cuts of some magnitude at the end of this school year, and even more cuts loomed for the upcoming year. And the bottom of the state's declining revenue picture not yet in sight. Facing such a problem, the superintendent knew that a systematic process was needed to (a) recommend budget cuts, (b) explain why each was recommended, and (c) create support for each and every recommendation. Such a process must involve representative stakeholders from district employees, all bargaining groups representing district employees, parents representing all school buildings and representatives for all administrators, at both the building and district levels. The process should seek ideas from everyone, judge all ideas against a common set of requirements, and all recommended cuts should fit within guidelines and assumptions agreed upon by all.

Since the district was a large district (approximately 37,000 students, 51 school buildings, 8 bargaining groups, and a large central office), the use of stakeholders from all levels and representing all interested groups meant that the systematic process would require a variety of committees and working groups. This created a rather detailed process involving a large number of people. A major concern might arise: Would this process work with small and medium sized districts? The authors of this text feel strongly that the answer is "Yes!" The process would be the same; only the complexity of the process and/or the size or number of the working groups would need to change.

Using the Process in Small or Medium Sized Districts

The first question a superintendent of a smaller district has to ask is, "Can this process be adapted to fit small and medium size districts?" The author's assurances should not suffice, if they stand alone and unsupported. A second question from a small medium sized district superintendent is also logical. Does the superintendent of a smaller district need to use a process involving numerous people? Could the same task be accomplished by using a small group of administrators? Here the authors feel the answer is "Yes," but not a simple yes. One must consider several issues when making the response.

The advantages of using this recommended process can be found at three distinctly different times, at three different stages of the process. Establishing the budget cutting process, identifying the basic assumptions to be used, and establishing guidelines for actions level the playing field for everyone involved *as the process begins*. Everyone agrees to use the same rules, to start with the same assumptions, and to move all suggestions through the same process. This immediately leads to a second benefit.

With a level playing field, (a) all ideas must be considered, (b) all ideas are examined by a group of stakeholders, and (c) everything culminates as a group makes the final recommendation(s). If group membership represents the total spectrum of special interest groups within the district, then everyone and every group is involved in and responsible for the final recommendation. No one person, no one group, and (especially) no one central office administrator is responsible for the recommended cuts. The superintendent is now surrounded with supporters for making each budget cut. Agreement already exists for what is cut, the size of each cut, and what is not cut. In board meetings all questions were directed to and answered by the chair of the group responsible for that specific recommendation. Recommendations and responses came from a committee. And since the committee making each recommendation for each specific cut had representatives from all interested groups, fewer questions were actually raised at board meetings. Interested parties already had their chance to discuss the changes, examine other possibilities, and reach consensus on a conclusion, all before the school board voted to approve or disapprove the specific recommendation.

The fact that a process was used to create the final recommendations yielded the third and final benefit. Late in any process to approve budget cuts, some individual or group (almost always representing personal or special interests) is bound to recommend changes. The appeal is always the same: "Don't make this cut; increase the cuts in other areas." Such late suggestions always come at awkward times: (1) When the school board package is being typed, (2) at a meeting where the board is to approve the final budget, or (3) after the final decision has been made.

Using a process makes the response to late suggestions obvious. *The process has to be used.* Since the late suggestion had not been through the process, most responses are simple: *Late ideas will not be considered; they have not been through the process.* But a door can always be left open: If the idea is really (1) original, (2) saves money, (3) seems to be a positive, and (4) seems to represent an idea for the district's good, a final decision can be delayed in order to "move the suggestion through the budget cutting process." In truth, however, an idea "representing forces for good" is rarely found at the board meeting called to approve the final budget package.

Clearly, the three benefits described above strongly suggest that districts of all sizes can benefit from using a budget cutting process, one that involves stakeholders throughout the entire district, rather than relying upon central office administrators to make all budget cutting recommendations. And, of course, there is always one other important reason for using a process involving many people: *Not all good ideas stem from one source.* Collecting ideas from a variety of people, having a variety of people discuss the impact of each idea, and having a group of people create the final package of recommendations, all assure that ideas are solicited at every stage in the process from numerous people representing a variety of stakeholders. In other words, nothing ever comes from a single source. And when the process is completed, every idea with merit has been suggested, considered, and included in the final package.

But the best way to (1) show how the process works and (2) that it works for smaller districts is to create a case study in this manual to demonstrate how suggested worksheets are used, how data are evaluated, and how recommendations stem from the process and work efforts completed in that process.

School District B: Budget Crisis Background and Facts

School District B is found in a town of approximately 12,000 people, but with a large area of small to medium sized family farms surrounding the town. The district enrolls approximately 5,000 students in six K-5 schools, a sixth grade center, one middle school, and one high school. The central office is located in an old school on property adjoining the sixth grade center. The central office uses only the first floor; second story rooms are utilized for special programs.

The credit collapse of 2008 had a major impact in the district's state. Tax collections were down; funding from the state level was being cut. A 3 percent holdback, requested during the 2008-2009 school year, was made permanent. State legislators debated additional reductions in school funding. They were approved. Several specific recommendations and/or requirements were attached to the final draft of the school funding bills. Support for transportation was being cut. A bill to allow reductions in teacher salaries and administrator salaries was recommended and passed. Lottery funds were moved into the general fund rather than being reserved for building construction and maintenance.

For District B these cuts were major. One of the six elementary schools is located some distance from town; therefore, transportation expenses to bring older children into the town are sizeable. A cut in state support for bus purchases and daily transportation expenses hit District B hard. The reduction in salaries, required by the state, also restricted the ability of the district to manage where and how budget cuts were made. The "one size fits all" approach taken by the state legislators did not take into account the different needs of districts. (Example: Transportation cuts hit District B hard, and the reductions in teacher salary support were troublesome.) District B is located near one of the state's major universities. While that means District B has always had ample teacher applications, it also means teachers don't resign. The average salary was well over the "average teacher salary level" funded by the state. This stems from two facts: most teachers have many years of experience and most have advanced degrees.

Finally, one other source of revenue seemed limited. A neighboring school district asked voters to approve a large supplemental levy to replace lost state revenues. That levy was soundly defeated well before District B voters were asked to vote on their supplemental levy. Therefore, the levy submitted to District B voters was reduced slightly. District B argued that it was asking for slightly less in local taxes, due to difficult economic times. Local voters responded favorably to this argument; the smaller supplemental levy was approved. But it was definitely smaller.

The superintendent of District B feared he was facing a major budget crisis. It looked as if the operating budget for the next year would be reduced by over 10 percent. But there was no reduction in the number of students, transportation costs were increasing again, and the state's head of public instruction insisted that all his new programs ideas move forward despite funding cuts. The superintendent of District B also knew (from speaking with legislators) that additional cuts were projected for the next two budget years. The budget cuts his district faced would not be a "one and done" experience.

For the superintendent a new budget had to be prepared for board approval soon after the final state budget figures were to be approved by the state legislature. So, trying to think ahead, he considered that it might be time to declare the fact that a budget crisis existed. Using a process to deal with required cuts, and to define possible areas for future budget cuts, would be vital. It was time for such a process to be created. And so, he turned to a worksheet from the budget cutting process to ascertain the severity of the district's problem. The worksheet is shown on the next page.

Several facts emerged from the superintendent's analysis of his budget figures. First, the actual reduction from the state did not appear to be large. But hidden in the figures was the fact that lottery funds, once reserved for building construction and remodeling, had been rolled over into the basic budget. This rollover hid a half million dollar reduction in his budget. Secondly, over $200,000 of the reserve account has been used this year, and if the district's budget was to remain in the black and spending was even close to the 2008-2009 level, approximately $800,000 would be used from the reserve account. At this rate, the reserve account will be totally depleted by the end of 2011.

Step 1: Situational Analysis: Identify District 827 Budget Crisis				
	Budget History by Year		Budget Projections by Year	
Revenue Sources	2007-2008 Amount	2008-2009 Amount	2009-2010 Amount	2010-2011 Amount
State Revenue Sources				
State Appropriation	20,199,131	21,026,299	20,766,770	19,728,431
Lottery Funds	516,255	492,706	0	0
Other State	761,733	691,244	668,563	635,135
Agriculture Exempt Tax	61,502	53,349	35,565	23,828
	21,538,621	22,263,598	21,470,898	20,387,394
Local Revenue Sources				
Fund Balance (Unencumbered)	1,156,000	1,901,340	1,700,000	900,000
Supplemental Levy	1,975,000	1,975,000	1,975,000	1,975,000
Plant Faciility Levy	0	0	0	0
Bond Levy	869,741	796,878	815,000	815,000
Misc: (Rentals)	21,491	24,600	24,600	24,600
Earning on Investments	324,723	153,800	100,000	95,000
General Taxes	80,519	0	0	0
		4,851,618	4,614,600	3,809,600
Federal Revenue Sources				
Impact Aid	1,076,938	501,217	635,000	620,000
Other Revenue Sources				
Medicaid	253,857	337,380	375,000	400,000
E-Rate/Misc	303,372	196,600	220,600	220,000

If nothing is done now, the superintendent reasoned, the reserve account will cover reduced allocations for two years. But that simply delays the budget crisis until 2011, and it would be much worse. The superintendent could hope for additional state dollars in two years, but all economic predictors indicated that real dollar growth in tax collections was several years away. The last predictions given to superintendents indicated the state's economy would not totally recover until 2015. This projection was in line with federal projections that it would take several years to recover from the recession of 2008.

It might be better to face the crisis now, with money still left in the reserve account, than to wait until that entire fund was gone. This seemed especially wise, as other state funding sources, including the agricultural inclusion money, were also being reduced. In two years the district would receive approximately $2,000,000 less from the state, the reserve account would be depleted, and no other revenue source seemed to be available to replace lost dollars. But expenses would be higher; inflation assures that. The superintendent's conclusion: Assuming some inflation, additional costs in teacher salaries, and or benefits, higher prices for transportation, etc., the actual reduction of almost 10 percent in state dollars could be closer to 15 percent in real dollars. With that reduction the district faced real financial problems.

Step 1: Identify District B Enrollment Situation				
	Enrollment History by Year		Enrollment Projections	
Enrollment by Schools	2007-2008 Enrollment	2008-2009 Enrollment	2009-2010 Enrollment	2010-2011 Enrollment
High School Enrollments				
High School (F - Sr)	1,680	1,685	1,691	1,652
Alternative High School	42	72	82	73
Subtotal	1,722	1,757	1,773	1,725
Middle/Junior High School				
Middle School (Gr 7 & 8)	810	821	809	793
Middle School (6th Gr)	406	410	398	377
Special Mid/Jr High 1	40	51	61	71
Subtotal	1,256	1,282	1,268	1,241
Elementary School				
Elementary School 1 (K-5)	372	366	355	342
Elementary School 2 (K-3)	253	234	221	196
Elementary School 3 (1-5)	318	310	341	362
Elementary School 4 (1-5)	322	323	302	288
Elementary School 5 (4-5)	207	215	201	207
Elementary School 6 (1-5)	375	356	340	331
Subtotal	1,847	1,804	1,760	1,726
Other Schools				
Kindergarten Center	220	214	201	223
Total Enrollment	5,045	5,057	5,002	4,915

What about enrollment? The superintendent created the chart to see what his enrollment trends were. He observed that there are presently more students in the upper grades and fewer in the lowest grades. There are more students per grade level in high school than in the elementary schools. However, one elementary school (#3) is growing; he knew a large housing development was under construction in that school's attendance area. That school is nearly filled; boundary changes will be needed in order to reduce the population of that school, and to maintain full classrooms in some of the surrounding schools.

The superintendent summarized his data. *The overall enrollment pattern is steady; the district does not project any sizeable reductions in the school population until 2011; by then two largest classes in the district will have graduated, and two smaller kindergarten classes will be enrolled. The district will receive less money from the state for the next two years based upon enrolment; and, of course, the larger of the two enrollment drops will occur for the 2011 school year, the same year the largest budget cuts in state funding are predicted. The district will, no doubt, have a retirement or two from the ranks of elementary school teachers in the next two years; it appears that some of those vacant lines can be left unfilled. Secondary retirements could be more difficult. A math or English teacher would have to be replaced. Electives can be cut, but with NCLB the basic math and language courses must be taught, and remedial classes or tutoring programs might be needed to ensure that graduation rates are met.*

His conclusion: *My district has a budget crisis.*

Required Board Actions

At the conclusion of some chapters, recommendations for school board actions will be given, as needed or whenever required. The purpose for these recommendations is singular: If a budget reduction process is to be created, the school board should be involved in every step of the process. They must approve the creation of such a process; they should approve the steps of the process. And final approval for all budget reduction suggestions is much more likely to occur if the school board has been informed and/or involved at every step.

The superintendent of District B was ready to ask the school board to approve a plan to "create a budget cutting process." Unless there was a dramatic change in the state's economy, it appeared District B would have less money for the upcoming year and much less money two years out.

Reference

DePree, Max. Retrieved November 5, 2009 from www.DailyQuotes.com.

Section II

Leadership in a Fiscal Crisis

Chapter Four

Leadership in Times of Financial Uncertainty

Nothing tests a leader like a crisis. There is an element of the leader's deepest character
that is revealed during highly charged, dramatic events. (Klann 2003)

Chapter Assumptions: Three assumptions serve as the foundation for this chapter.
1. Leadership behavior and action during a financial crisis relies primarily upon the effective use of influence in pursuit of a common goal.
2. Leadership actions in a financial crisis are different than other crises because any financial crisis is usually predictable.
3. A set of leadership principles applicable for any financial crisis can be predetermined and implemented.

Chapter Objectives:
1. Identify essential leadership principles for financial uncertainty.
2. Describe the role and actions of the leader during financial uncertainty.

Leadership Introduction

A school crisis of any kind is, at best, an extremely difficult situation for the leader of the school district. Conversations with superintendents who have experienced a major crisis event indicate the experience had a significant impact on their careers. Some rethought their career goals. Others markedly changed their leadership style and practice. In every instance those superintendents stated the crisis experience tested their leadership and management skills in a multitude of different ways.

During the crisis the superintendents were busy reacting to the crisis event; reacting almost always means managing the crisis within whatever policies and practices the school district already had that dealt with the crisis event. For most of these crisis events, however, the superintendent had little or no time for preparation: the crisis just occurred. In such events, superintendents had to manage the district's response within existing policies. In such crisis events, superintendents use the best possible management practices to react to the crisis, but they are still reacting. The event itself dictates most of what is said, done, or reported.

But financial uncertainty in a financial crisis presents a totally different situation. Why? Financial uncertainty is predictable; over the last forty years virtually every decade has included times of fiscal uncertainty. Fortunately, many of the economic disruptions in the last forty or fifty years were relatively short lived. But the main point should be obvious. Armed with the knowledge that periods of financial uncertainty are bound to occur, a superintendent should use his/her leadership skills in advance to build processes that prepare a school district for financial uncertainty and to deal immediately and responsibly with the inevitable financial crisis. Financial crises are bound to occur; that is axiomatic. But in the response to a crisis, leaders vary.

Effective leadership practices help a school district (a) be prepared for times of financial uncertainty, and if economic events turn fiscal uncertainty into a financial crisis, the advance preparation (b) helps the district manage a fiscal crisis more effectively. Applying leadership skills, first to create a system and then to implement it when managing the fiscal crisis, is important for one major reason. A financial crisis can create lasting problems; financial crises may have a long life span. For example, experts suggest the nationwide financial problems of 2007 could impact government budgets for three to five years. In other words, a superintendent might face budget cuts, one on top of another, for three to five years. The first budget cuts might be easy; but if the district faces cuts in subsequent budgets, each additional budget reduction is more difficult to face and even more difficult to achieve.

One important point should be repeated for emphasis. Financial crises are bound to occur. There were economic downturns in the 1970s, 1980s, and 1990s; each impacted school budgets in negative ways. They may have varied in impact and severity, but economic and/or budget issues occurred during each of those decades. The economic problems of 2007 and 2008 were much more severe; these economic events could definitely move a district from mild problems associated with "financial uncertainty" to "a major budget crisis." But regardless of the severity, each new economic downturn can be viewed as another bump in a long line of financial ups and downs. The conclusion is obvious. Given the reoccurring nature of financial problems, effective leadership practice demands that a superintendent have a process in place to help manage "bad times."

A second fact should also be obvious. Financial crises force superintendents and other schools administrators to manage the crisis. In creating a process in advance for use during tough times, everyone who makes the tough decisions has a process to use, a process offering guidance and support. This should be helpful to everyone in managing the crisis. How helpful? To be blunt, a financial crisis often determines differences between effective leaders and ex-leaders.

During any actual fiscal crisis, however, a superintendent must lead and manage. Leadership and management, in tough financial times, can be viewed as two ways of facing the same problem. Klann (2003), in his book *Crisis Leadership*, distinguishes between crisis management and crisis leadership as follows: "I would differentiate the two by saying that crisis management relates mainly to operational issues, while crisis leadership principally deals with how leaders handle the human response" (p. ix). But make no mistake: both management and leadership are necessary during a crisis. The key difference between crisis management and crisis leadership, according to Klann, is influence.

> Influence is the ability to persuade, convince, motivate, inspire, and judiciously use power to effect others in a positive way. . . . The difference lies not in the importance of influence as a leadership capacity but rather in the particular conduct of the crisis itself, an emotional cauldron that distills the components of influence into a potent concentration of three key elements: communication, clarity of vision and values, and caring. (pp. 11-12)

The superintendent and senior leadership of a school district must recognize that a crisis of financial uncertainty is atypical of other crises. In general, it threatens the ability of the district to perform its primary mission as required by society. This type of crisis threatens not only the district, but also the very livelihood of its employees. Similarly, it creates in parents and/or guardians severe concern about the educational opportunities provided to children. And finally, particularly in small communities, there is a negative impact on local businesses whenever district employees reduce spending.

The superintendent, as the leader of a large institution and a large employer in any community, must serve as the exemplar for (a) behaviors, (b) language, and (c) caring expected of all district leadership personnel during a financial crisis. Superintendents set expectations; the superintendent's direct reports must transmit these expectations to everyone across the district. This emphasizes transmitting the same expectations to every department, every school, and every member of the community at large.

(Author's Note: In writing this manual the authors have tried to avoid educational jargon as much as possible. But jargon can be helpful when a word or phrase replaces several words, or even line of print with a single word or phrase. The authors have chosen to use a phrase that can be construed as educational jargon, but it is useful. So, the phrase "direct reports" will refer to school administrators who report directly to the superintendent. Such individuals might also be described as being part of the district leadership team.)

Essential Leadership Principles during Financial Uncertainty

What are the specific leadership principles that the superintendent must employ during a crisis of financial uncertainty? The following are usually essential; other principles might be added.
1. A clear communication strategy that articulates the exact nature of the crisis.
2. Reinforcement of the district vision and underlying values communicated in a manner that encourages commitment and ownership by all employees, especially the senior leadership team.
3. A system of caring support for employees that recognizes the emotional turmoil they are encountering and promotes the importance of the job they are doing.
4. A commitment to a collaborative leadership process.
5. Enhance trust in district leadership by doing what you say you will do.
6. Demonstrate a commitment to solving the crisis with a personal sacrifice.
7. Establish guiding principles, both for decision-making and for making timely decisions.
8. Aggressively pursue proactive rather than reactive planning when addressing the crisis.

The leadership principles employed during a crisis of financial uncertainty may have been (a) developed prior to the crisis or (b) created specifically for the crisis. Regardless of their origin, it is vital that all plans, decisions, preventative actions, etc., be based on these principles. Whether the crisis occurs in a small, medium, or large school district, these principles are critical to those individuals in leadership positions during that crisis. The superintendent must ensure that the principles are embedded in the day-to-day operation of the district as it faces the financial crisis.

The Role of the Leader during Financial Uncertainty

Essential for the superintendent during a crisis of financial uncertainty is embedding the leadership principles into the daily fabric of the school district. This is a major responsibility and the superintendent must be assured that his/her direct reports are committed to the principles. Without the commitment of direct reports to core leadership principles, each school employee, from administrator to teacher to staff member, is left to his/her own view of the crisis and each will act according to their own principles or goals.

While the superintendent's direct reports will undoubtedly have been involved in determining the list of leadership principles, there should be no question about one fact: The list begins and ends with the superintendent. As with most significant issues in a school district, the superintendent provides a guiding hand for the final decision, both in creating that decision and in enforcing that decision.

The recommended leadership principles suggested here are detailed in the following sections; for the purpose of this manual, each is addressed in relation to the role of the superintendent.

(1) The superintendent creates a clear communication strategy that articulates the crisis of financial uncertainty.

The message regarding the severity of the financial crisis should not be minimized. Since most, if not all, employees will be affected, timely, concise, and honest communication on the probabilities resulting from the crisis must be set forth. A strategy (see chapter 5) must be developed that addresses (a) the most immediate, (b) the most probable, and (c) the worst-case scenarios. This message must first be presented to the school board; it must be combined with the statement that failure is not an option.

The concern of "failure is not an option" should be emphasized. A school district cannot close its doors; children will need an education regardless of economic times. So, the following example is shown to make that point.

Schools Are Not a Business; Failure Is Not an Option

A national drug store chain had one store in a community of 65,000. During a period of three years, two large national retail corporations decided to build "superstores" in the community. Each more than doubled the square footage of existing stores to create huge retail outlets selling groceries, drugs, furniture, home furnishings, clothing, sporting equipment, toys, and automotive supplies. At this point a national drug store chain decided to build two additional stores in the town. Simply stated, they could not compete with the superstores. Little more than a year after the new buildings were completed, both were closed. Within another year, the original store was closed. Evidently, the drug store chain could write off the loss, sell or lease the new buildings, and move on. School districts do not have that option. A town's schools cannot be boarded up and closed just because administrators or managers did not adequately face and adapt to a financial crisis.

Similarly, command, control and coordination of all communications must be centered in the superintendent's office, either with the superintendent personally (as is usually the case in a small district) or with an individual closely aligned with the superintendent. The communication strategy's purpose must be to influence the behavior of district employees in a manner that results in their commitment to the process the district must use to solve the financial crisis.

(2) The district's leadership team has a vision statement and a list of underlying values that are communicated to encourage commitment to and ownership by all district employees and patrons.

Klann (2003) emphasizes this point by stating, "Having a clear vision and values system (either personal or passed down from the organization) that can be communicated so direct reports understand it, feel ownership of it, and endorse it is a powerful tool before, during, and after a crisis," p. 14. This leadership principle affords the superintendent a golden opportunity to review and remind direct reports of the key values that serve as the foundation of the district's mission. Establishing time to reinforce this message is essential in all efforts used to mitigate the financial crisis. Listening to the views and concerns of the direct reports in this process is important, as their views and concerns usually reflect those whom they supervise.

The district's vision statement and underlying values form the basis for making all financial decisions. And most importantly, once a meeting of the minds is reached on this fact, the agreed upon message must be supported by all, without exception!

(3) The superintendent creates a system of caring support for employees that recognizes the emotional turmoil they are encountering and promotes the importance of the job they are doing and demonstrates confidence that working together the district will weather the financial crisis.

A high degree of stress and tension is usually exhibited in those individuals most intimately involved with the crisis, in this instance, teachers, principals, and all district employees. This can result in employees deciding they have little or no control over the crisis and thus, in the vernacular, they feel powerless and unvalued. Support and caring are vital for those who must help solve the problem.

A high degree of effort is needed in times of financial crisis to survive the crisis while still meeting the needs of students. People will work hard in any crisis, but in times of financial crisis it is usually impossible to reward such behavior with pay. Therefore, emotional and/or social support systems are vital to assure everyone continues working on difficult tasks in a positive manner. Negativity is often present in difficult times; keeping everyone positive and stopping negative role-players is vital. Consider the impact the following role players might have on the problem solving process.

Negative Role Player Examples (And What to Do About Them!)

Bunker Man: This individual hunkers down, avoids involvement in the problem solving process, and waits out the storm. Action: People who hide from the problem are not needed.

Fight Man: My budget cannot be cut; everything I do is vital to the district's mission. Find your cuts elsewhere. Action: People who can't make cuts are replaced by those who can.

Flight Man: If you cut my budget, it means my work is not appreciated here. Maybe I should move on. Action: Accept the resignation.

Even though the superintendent and the direct reports will be sufficiently engaged addressing the financial uncertainty with consideration of potential budget cuts, communicating with the school board, and other important activities, they must not ignore the need to be highly visible throughout the district. This visibility must be well thought out and designed to support employee efforts to continue performing their jobs in a positive manner. Visibility can be achieved by the superintendent and direct reports visiting classrooms, riding a bus to or from a school, serving lunch at a school, attending a faculty meeting, speaking to a parent group, having lunch with the maintenance staff, meeting monthly with a group of principals on their territory, meet with students, etc. These activities or events offer substantial opportunity to praise the work employees are doing and to reinforce the districts mission and fundamental values. Remember, every employee, to some degree, is uncertain about their future and their ability to provide for their family or significant other. The goal of this leadership principle is to share the importance of district values and give employees a positive reason to come to work each day with confidence they are essential to the mission of the district.

(4) The superintendent demonstrates a commitment to a collaborative leadership process.

One individual cannot solve the financial crisis. Although there are those who believe the superintendent is the only one who can address the solution to the crisis and should be the only one held accountable for success or failure. This is an overly simplistic view of the situation, at best. Every employee should be offered an opportunity to participate in solving the crisis (See chapter 10), and collaborative processes should be designed, implemented, and monitored. This goes to the heart of how the leader, the superintendent, views his role, either as the top-down decision-maker, or a facilitator of a process to obtain as much assistance as possible to solve the financial crisis. Fundamentally, the collaborative process recognizes the superintendent cannot do it alone, and others may have ideas worth considering. Ultimately, if given the opportunity to participate in the solution to the crisis, a stronger commitment to the eventual solution will result.

Style and Substance

The process of collaboration should be seen as the heart and soul of this manual. This point can be illustrated by the following: Everyone has met leaders who give lip service to the style of collaboration. They talk of shared decision-making, collaborative work efforts, and team building. But when it is only style that is considered, decisions are made at the top, group recommendations are ignored, and collaboration is non-existent. Fewer have met leaders who believe in the substance of collaboration. Substance means that shared decisions are the decision, collaborative work efforts yield final products, and teams are built to complete jobs. Delegation is real. Substance means that policies are made through cooperation and collaboration; administrators can enforce such policies individually, but they do not make the policies individually. When dealing with a budget crisis, the administrator making all decisions stands alone. But the administrator using a collaborative process should be surrounded by supporters when the final plans are presented for approval.

(5) The superintendent works to enhance trust in district leadership by using the principle of "Doing what you say you will do." Two major points should be made about this principle.

Trust is difficult to obtain and easy to lose. This point is obvious; little needs to be added. The superintendent seeking the trust and respect of everyone involved with the school district and its budget crisis must work constantly to earn and maintain trust. The character of an individual is the foundation for the trust others give. Perhaps the only way that trust can be earned and maintained is when the superintendent acts in accordance with his/her basic character traits during the crisis. Klann (2003) states:

> Synonymous with integrity, this trait of conscious moral behavior defines who you are when no one is watching. At a minimum, character implies telling the truth, being consistent in word and deed, treating people with dignity, avoiding actions that even hint at impropriety, and exercising self-control in the areas of morality and self-discipline, p. 16.

(6) The superintendent demonstrates a commitment to solving the crisis with a personal sacrifice.

Ethical behavior begins at the top of every effective organization. In the case of a superintendent reducing his salary by 5 percent (see chapter 2 for an example of applying ethical leadership to a practical situation) the superintendent sacrificing a benefit, monetary or not, sends a clear message the crisis of financial uncertainty is serious. An illustration is provided in the following:

District A: The Superintendent's First Action

The superintendent of a large city school district determined that a 20 percent revenue shortfall over a twelve month period would severely hamper the ability of the district to provide a quality education to the students they were charged with serving. The superintendent realized decisive action was necessary to galvanize district employees and the community to action. His decision was to announce an immediate 5 percent reduction in his annual salary. Further, he obtained the commitment of non-bargaining employees to reduce their annual salaries by 3 percent. The personal sacrifice by the superintendent and the other employees signified the dramatic impact financial uncertainty would have on the district.

Fortunately, the aforementioned action of the school district's leader caught the attention of the bargaining groups representing the remainder of district employees. Further, the actions drew praise from community leaders, the print and television media, and the state legislature. The results were exactly what the superintendent desired.

As a result of the superintendent's actions, representatives of the bargaining groups signaled they were willing to discuss salary issues in the interest of saving jobs. They also indicated that they wished to participate in the budget cutting process and to address actions necessary to solve the fiscal crisis. In this district the actions of the superintendent spoke louder than any words that could have been spoken; they helped get the attention of all district's stakeholders. When the superintendent volunteered to take a pay cut, it signaled to everyone involved that the financial crisis was real, serious and immediate. It also signaled that no one could be above the process. The signal was obvious: If the boss takes a pay cut as step one, it must be serious!

One limitation should be put on the idea of signals. It is described in the following example, with illustrations to show the variety of efforts that might be made and an example of choosing the sacrifice to actually match the perceived problem.

District A: Fitting the Sacrifice to the Situation

Not every budget crisis situation should be met with the same public demonstration. Consider the following possible reactions a superintendent might take in order to demonstrate a problem is serious enough to impact his/her own compensation package.

1. Giving Up Attending a National Meeting: When budget cuts are small, a small or symbolic demonstration may show that everyone needs to make small cuts.
2. Turning Down a District Car: When times are more difficult, turning down a fringe benefit shows the leader is willing to make larger sacrifices.
3. Taking a Pay Cut: As shown in the example given above, severe problems must be met with a sacrifice of some magnitude.

The point of this example is obvious. When the leader and the leadership team members demonstrate a willingness to recommend and take personal benefit cuts, everyone is more willing to make sacrifices for the common goal.

---

(7) The superintendent leads in establishing a set of guiding principles for both decision-making and assuring those decisions are made in a timely manner.

Many different authors state support for establishing basic, guiding principles for decision-making. Individual school districts must create their set of recommendations to serve a foundation. These should already exist. In dealing with a budget crisis Gaufin (2006) makes a major point: "It's never too early to prepare." Leaders, particularly in a crisis, can't wait for every piece of information before deciding on a course of action. But they should have, and rely upon, a framework within which critical decisions will be made. The authors have chosen to call this framework the guiding principles. They are outlined in detail in chapter 7.

The fundamental key to the guiding principles framework is that some guidance and parameters are required in the fast moving environment of a crisis, in this instance, financial uncertainty for the district. The guiding principles selected by the superintendent and direct reports depend upon the local situation. However, regardless of the local environment, to operate without adhering to a set of guiding principles any decision will do. Careful thought must be undertaken to determine the guiding principles that will best serve the environment in which the crisis of financial uncertainty occurs.

(8) The superintendent aggressively pursues proactive rather than reactive planning in the crisis.

Planning before, during, and after a financial crisis is essential for a school district. Most economic downturns are predictable as is evidenced by the downturns in the 1970s, 1980s, 1990s, and the most recent fiscal crisis across the United States. Therefore, the superintendent should be able to plan ahead for what might happen if there is a substantial revenue shortfall during a school year, or from one year to the next. But such planning should not be seen as preparing for the negative. Good planning includes knowing where the district is, where it wants to be, and what is required both to (a) keep it going and (b) move it forward, and is as useful for spending more money as it is useful for spending less money.

Establish a Budget Reduction Process

Essential to addressing any complex problem is to recognize that complex problems demand complex solutions. The authors of this manual will never recommend quick fix solutions. The across the board cuts model does not work when cuts are large. Similarly, simply assigning a target number for departmental cuts is not realistic. Neither of these simple solutions addresses such issues as "What is the mission of the district?" and "How do we sustain that mission in hard times?" Instead, the authors of this text recommend a "systems approach" to budget planning for difficult times, one that reflects Klann's (2003) point about systematic planning. Consider Klann's opinion: "Leaders of vision anticipate the possibility of a crisis and know that when a crisis hits it is far too late to plan, and, even worse, it is virtually impossible to respond effectively without a plan in place", p. 75.

The six-step budget reduction process described in this manual has been designed to address budget concerns before they occur. The superintendent who engages in proactive planning understands that good times do not go on forever; sooner or later, everyone will face financial emergencies. Therefore, a process for budgeting in difficult times should be in place. The six steps recommended here are:

1. Situational analysis: "Where are we at now?"
2. Establishing strategic direction: "What are district priorities?"
3. Idea generation: "Brainstorm all possibilities from all stakeholders."
4. Idea analysis: "Which ideas will work for our district?"
5. Staff and community evaluation: "Build consensus for decision-making."
6. School board review and action: "Board commits to recommended cuts."

Determine Base Quality Education

A critical companion to this leadership principle is to always know what district programs, practices, and services serve as the foundation of district operations. This can be effectively achieved by determining if programs and/or services meet one or more of the following criteria:

1. Required by established standards.
2. Referenced in established standards as highly desirable.
3. No standard is available although highly desirable.
4. No required standard is available and appropriate.

The leadership of a school district should continually update district program documents (all laws, requirements, recommendations, etc.) that impact requirements so that effective planning for the future can be undertaken without delays.

Obviously, such documentation is also vital when planning for an immediate crisis. In other words, knowing what is required for the district's base quality education program should always be available and on file. As laws or standards or requirements or recommendations change, these basic documents must be updated. The differences between state laws or board policies and recommended standards should always be clear in such documentation.

The purpose of such documentation is to define the district's base quality education program. This requires that the district define its (a) base quality education program and (b) the essential support services. In other words, what is required in each of the district's elementary, middle, or senior high schools in terms of library books, teacher student ratios, technology equipment, textbooks, aides, or any other variable that might be mentioned in any legal document or standards of professional organizations? Defining the base quality education program and essential support services at any and every school level in the district helps determine how new money or less money should be spent.

Several worksheets are provided at the end of this chapter; they are included to provide guidance to district senior leadership team members for defining the base quality educational program of the district. A more detailed examination of the base quality educational program will be presented in later chapters.

Proactive Planning and Budget Reductions

The primary impediment to preparing advanced plans for financial uncertainty is the belief by many district leaders that most financial crises will be avoided by the educational system. Further, some superintendent's view planning as a hindrance to their ability to react to the changing nature of the political arena, legislative action, and the requirements placed on educators. Finally, some believe that creating a plan for operating the district with less money is an indirect statement that the district actually needs less money. Obviously, the authors of this manual do not share any of these beliefs. The need to plan for financial uncertainty is as critical as having a plan for any other emergency. Attacks upon schools and/or students have shown that plans were needed for the safety and security of students who might be threatened by outside sources. The economic upturns and downturns of the past thirty years should emphasize for all that advanced budget planning is as important as creating plans for dealing with emergency or student safety concerns.

There are critical steps to preparing a sound financial plan for school district use during a crisis of financial uncertainty. District employees and members of the community expect the superintendent to find a way to continue the educational programs essential to preparing students for the future. The key steps in this planning effort are the foundation of this manual and are explained in detail in later chapters. For this basic administrative principle, one point is key.

Planning is a proactive activity. Reacting to a crisis of financial uncertainty limits the ability of the superintendent and the school board to either make decisions or influence the overall decision-making process. People do not always make sound decisions under duress; the differing pressures and influences concerning time, money, publicity, and special interests do not sort themselves out in difficult times. One other fact supports the need for proactive planning. To ignore sound proactive planning needs presents the real possibility that a district could face several minor financial crises without sound plans. Putting employees and the community through a series of "repeat crises" is irresponsible at best; at the worst, it raises questions about how many times can a district cry "Wolf!" before cooperation ceases and self-interests rule decision-making. Effective planning can and should help serve to stabilize the district during one crisis or repeated crises, thus enabling all decisions to be made according to the plans and/or criteria laid out in the planning documents.

The need for proactive planning is present in both good times and hard times. Having proactive plans in place helps the superintendent lead. As a result, in both good times and hard times,

The message is simple: "Plan your work and work your plan."

References

Gaufin, Joyce (2006). *Key principles for effective crisis leadership (PPT)*. Retrieved August 10, 2009. www.health.utah.gov/leadership.

Klann, Gene (2003). *Crisis leadership, using military lessons, organizational experiences, and the power of influence to lesson the impact of chaos on the people you lead*. Greensboro, NC: Center for Creative Leadership, p. 1.

Chapter 4 Worksheets

Leadership in Times of Financial Uncertainty

Tough times require real leadership.

Part A
Establish Standards for Base Quality Education

Part B
Seven Leadership Principles for Consideration in Budget Reductions

Base Quality Education

To ensure that budget reductions do not destroy the instructional program of your school or district, we must have a definition of what is the base quality the district must sustain despite the reveue shortfall. The first base quality definition must deal with instructional issues.

Elementary Schools:			Required		Desirable	
What should base quality education program include or provide?			Rrequired by State Law	Establlished Standards	Desired, No Standards	Not Required
I		Direct Instruction				
A		Classroom Teachers				
B		Special Education Teachers				
C		Content Area Teachers				
	1	Physical Ed				
	2	Music				
D		Curriculum Materials and Textbooks				
	1	Reading				
	2	Mathematics				
	3	Language Arts				
	4					
E						
II		Indirect Instruction				
A		Library				
	1	Librarian				
	2	Books Per Student				
B						
III		Direct Support Services				
A		Teacher Aide				
	1	Kindergarten				
	2	Special Education				
B						
IV		Indirect Support Services				
A		Transportation				
B						
C						

Base Quality Education

To ensure that budget reductions do not destroy the instructional program of your school or district, we must have a definition of what is the base quality the district must sustain despite the reveue shortfall. The first base quality definition must deal with instructional issues.

Middle/Junior High Schools:			Required		Desirable	
What should base quality education program include/provide?			Rrequired by State Law	Establlished Standards	Desired, No Standards	Not Required
I		Direct Instruction				
	A	Required Content Area Teachers				
		1 Mathematics				
		2 Language Arts				
	B	Suggested Content Area Teachers				
		1 Physical Ed				
		2 Music				
	C	Special Education Teachers				
	D	Curriculum Materials and Textbooks				
	E					
II		Indirect Instruction				
	A	Library				
		1 Librarian				
		2 Books Per Student				
	B					
III		Direct Support Services				
	A	Teacher Aide				
		1 Remedial Reading				
		2 Special Education				
	B					
IV		Indirect Support Services				
	A	Transportation				
	B					
	C					

Base Quality Education

To ensure that budget reductions do not destroy the instructional program of your school or district, we must have a definition of what is the base quality the district must sustain despite the reveue shortfall. The first base quality definition must deal with instructional issues.

Senior High Schools:		Required		Desirable	
What should base quality education program include/provide?		Rrequired by State Law	Establlished Standards	Desired, No Standards	Not Required
I	Direct Instruction				
A	Required Content Area Teachers				
1	Mathematics				
2	Language Arts				
B	Suggested Content Area Teachers				
1	Physical Ed				
2	Music				
C	Special Education Teachers				
D	Curriculum Materials and Textbooks				
E					
II	Indirect Instruction				
A	Library				
1	Librarian				
2	Books Per Student				
B					
III	Direct Support Services				
A	Teacher Aide				
1	Remedial Reading				
2	Special Education				
B					
IV	Indirect Support Services				
A	Transportation				
B					
C					

Leadership Worksheet Section

General Statements

In times of crisis, leaders are either born or dismissed. Success comes when leaders step up, focus on primary concerns, make controversial decisions, and generally *Lead*! In crisis times those who focus on minutiae are minimized; those who focus on identifying key problems and finding solutions to those problems are maximized.

So superintendents facing financial woes should step back and ask:
1. What are the key leadership principles I wish to stress during this crisis?
2. What behaviors do I expect from myself? Of my leadership team?
3. How can I find consensus for the decisions that must be made?
4. How can I avoid contentious debates and self-serving decision-making?

The following worksheets are offered as a starting point; such a group of worksheets can be added to, modified, or otherwise changed by the leader. But the key point remains:

The effective leader in a crisis is one who (a) identifies the problem, (b) ascertains the components important to himself or herself, and (c) then brings his or her personal strengths, individual and collective leadership team strengths, and a variety of community assets together to focus on the problem's solution. Nitpicking on details, infighting over power, protecting domains, or valuing process over solutions will not solve problems. Leaders identify what has to be done, define how it should be done, and encourage all individuals or groups to take part in the process of doing; it is all done to arrive at workable solutions to the budget crisis. Such leaders succeed in crisis times.

Consider the following eight worksheets as possible suggestions, possibilities for consideration, and encouragements for self-examination and self-evaluation. They are meant to be "things to think about" as you enter the crisis. What do you believe should be available; do you have it; must you develop it, and, when everything is present, how should they be used? Each worksheet stresses a leadership principle important in crisis situations.

You may wish to add others.

Leadership in Times of Financial Uncertainty

Directions: Check each column that applies to leadership decisions you make.

Essential Leadership Principle:		Develop	Draft Exists	Modify	Completed	Consensus	Approve Date	Comments
I	The superintendent has clearly commmunicated the severity of the financial crisis.							Printed copies ready for distribution
A	It has been agreed upon by all leadership team members.							
B	It clearly articulates the exact nature of the financial crisis.							
C	It details the immediate reduction needed for the financial crisis.							
D	It states the most probable level of the financial crisis.							Ready for Board Meeting
E	It describes the worst-case scenario of the crisis.							
F	A time frame exists for communicating financial crisis decisions and strategies to stakeholders.							Depends on discussion at next board meeting
1	School Board Members							
2	District Employees							
3	Parents							
4	Community Members							
5	The Media							
6	Others							

Directions: Check each column that applies to leadership decisions you make.

	Essential Leadership Principle:	Develop	Draft Exists	Modify	Completed	Consensus	Approve Date	Comments
II	The leadership team agrees to use the district vision and mission statements as a foundation for addressing financial crises.							
A	Endorsement of the vision and mission statements recommended to:							
1	School Board							
2	Building Administrators							
3	Teachers							
4	Classified Staff							
5	Community Stakeholders							
B	All documents prepared will address application of vision and mission statements.							
C	All stakeholder meetings reinforce or apply vision and mission principles.							

Directions: Check column that applies to leadership decision you wish to make.

	Essential Leadership Principle:	Develop	Draft Exists	Modify	Completed	Consensus	Approve Date	Comments
III	A enhanced recognition plan exists to reinforce significant stakeholder contributions to their job or the school district.							
A	Senior leadership team members will increase their visibility in the workplace and community.							
B	A consistent message is delivered by all school officials during public activities.							
C	The adopted plan includes special recognition for over and above contributions.							
1	Administrators							
2	Teachers							
3	Instructional Assistants							
4	Support Staff							
5	Parents							
6	Volunteers							
7	Community Members							

Directions: Check each column that applies to leadership decisions you make.

Essential Leadership Principle:		Develop	Draft Exists	Modify	Completed	Consensus	Approve Date	Comments
IV	The superintendent and leadership team are committed to engendering trust.							
A	Honesty will be demonstrated in all communication and actions during the crisis.							
B	The leadership team will model the concept of practicing what is preached.							
C	Agreeing to self check fellow team members regarding all actions meet this principle.							
D	Stakeholder representatives agree to adhere this principle in their actions.							
E	Periodically secure feedback from key stakeholders on all actions addressing the financial crisis.							

Directions: Check each column that applies to leadership decisions you make.

Essential Leadership Principle:		Develop	Draft Exists	Modify	Completed	Consensus	Approve Date	Comments
V	The superintendent is committed to the collaborative decision-making process to address the financial crisis.							
A	Senior leadership team members know and apply principles of collaborative							
B	A specific plan exists to address financial issues using collaborative decision-making processes.							
1	The school board supports the collaborative decision-making process.							
2	The first stakeholder meetings will establish the collaborative decision-making proccess.							
3	All subsequent stakeholder meetings will utilize the collaborative decision-making process.							

Directions: Check each column that applies to leadership decisions you make.

Essential Leadership Principle:	Develop	Draft Exists	Modify	Completed	Consensus	Approve Date	Comments
VI The superintendent has announced a personal monetary sacrifice to demonstrate the severity of the crisis.							
A The superintendent has requested each member of the leadership team to determine the personal sacrifice each will make.							
B The senior leadership team will meet and approve all individual sacrifices as being of equal value and equal visibility.							
C Each sacrifice must have an assigned monetary value.							
D The superintendent has also requested that all non-bargaining group employees submit their personal sacrifice plan.							
E The leadership team meets to approve the plans submitted by non-bargaining individuals, by group or job category.							
F If board members are compensated, the board will publically announce their sacrifice plan.							

Directions: Check each column that applies to leadership decisions you make.

Essental Leadership Principle:	Develop	Draft Exists	Modify	Completed	Consensus	Approve Date	Comments
VII The superintendent has proposed a general framework of principles to address the financial crisis.							
A The senior leadership team has deveoped a full draft of the guiding principles.							
B The guiding principles are viewed for suggested modifications by all stakeholder representatives.							
C The senior leadership finalizes, for board review, the recommended guiding							
D The school board receives, reviews, modifies, approves, and adopts the guiding principles.							
E The board approved guiding principles are distributed to and reviewed with all stakeholder representatives.							

Directions: Check each column that applies to leadership decisions you make.

	Approving the Complete Budget Reduction Process	Develop	Draft Exists	Modify	Completed	Consensus	Approve Date	Comments
VIII	The superintendent proposes a six step budget reduction process.							
A	The senior leadership team reviews, modifies and concurs with the six step budget reduction process.							
B	The complete budget reduction process is prepared for review, modification, and/or adoption by the school board.							
C	School board authorizes the superintendent to implement the final approved budget reduction plan.							
D	The superintendent and senior leadership team develop an implementation plan to inform all key stakeholders of the process.							
E	The plan is implemented and all stakeholders are made aware of their role and responsibilities within that process.							

Chapter Five

Communicating in Times of Financial Uncertainty

During a crisis people are often fearful about what has happened,
what will happen, and how the crisis will affect them. (Klann 2003)

Chapter Assumptions: Three basic assumptions form the foundation of this chapter.
1. Communication strategies for financial crises must be designed for the long term and for a broader audience than those for any single crisis event.
2. Communication principles during a financial crisis should be grounded in a commitment to collaborative leadership.
3. The superintendent should adopt a "no surprises" approach when establishing communication principles and strategies for a financial crisis.

Chapter Objectives: Three objectives form the base of this chapter.
1. Stress the need for creating effective communication strategies.
2. Identify essential communication principles for financial uncertainty.
3. Describe the leader's role in creating communication policies and strategies.

The Basis for Effective Communication Strategies

The opening quote succinctly describes the emotions of school district employees when they are faced with a financial crisis in their workplace. Unlike other crises, a financial crisis has the potential to extend over a long period of time. As a result, school district employees not only feel the initial shock of the crisis, but, when finally realizing the extent of a severe financial crisis, employees begin to recognize its possible long-term effects on their careers and family.

Historically, school districts have had to address reductions in funding for specific programs or services. State legislatures or the federal government have reduced a percentage of reimbursement for transportation, underfunded a mandated program, or revised a basic funding formula. Over time, any of these require that the school district redesign programs or service deliveries. While these financial difficulties may have caused the school district to adjust personnel hiring practices, curb some professional development, or in limited ways modify the program using such funds, the district as a whole did not experience the loss of funds. However, a major financial crisis that significantly (a) reduces state funding for the district, (b) decreases the revenue available locally, and (c) is projected to extend over several years can cause dramatic change for the entire school district.

Once a financial crisis is determined to impact the mission and operation of the entire district, the superintendent and senior leadership must begin to think, plan, communicate, and act with regard to a broader audience: the patrons of the entire district, not just those served by a single program. In this situation all categories of employees at every level of the district must be included in any communication program and strategies that address the crisis. In addition, the communitywide audience must be integrated into all efforts to effectively communicate the crisis and the steps necessary to address it.

A variety of questions need to be raised by the superintendent and senior leadership as they consider the communication strategies required to engage the various audiences in finding solutions to the financial crisis. A starter list of questions should include, but not be limited to, the following idea:

- How bad is the crisis?
- How and when should the school board be informed?
- Should all known information be shared with the various stakeholders?
- Is there a benefit to telling the stakeholders what to expect?
- Should total candor serve as the foundation of the communication strategy?
- Should different communication techniques be designed for each stakeholder group?
- How does the district continue to pursue its mission during the crisis?
- How will the district address the emotional turmoil and stress upon employees?
- Should various stakeholder groups be involved in identifying solutions to the crisis?
- What core values held by the district should be reinforced and supported to demonstrate commitment to students, employees, and parents?

The answers to these and other such questions should serve as the foundation for creating a communication plan to be used by the district. As noted in chapter 3, the first leadership principle during a major crisis is the creation of a clear communication strategy that articulates the exact nature of the crisis. Each of the seven remaining leadership principles must also be integrated into the overall communication plan. Underlying any communication plan must be the opportunity to adjust to different circumstances and allow for flexibility with implementation of the plan. The superintendent and senior leadership must trust each other to carry out the elements of the plan without an undo amount of bureaucratic interference.

Communication Strategies in Turbulent Times

The literature addressing best practices with crisis communication includes both recommendations and examples of effective strategies based on the military (Klann 2003), the health professions (Gaufin 2006), the ICON Project at the University of Maryland (Blum 2009), planning for the unthinkable (Mitroff 1999), and over 100 citations focused on crisis leadership and communication. This chapter cannot adequately describe or summarize the myriad points presented in the literature regarding crisis communication. However, the authors wish to suggest and/or emphasize a few salient points gleaned over time by the authors. These points, coupled with the authors' experience in real life situations, should provide guidance to superintendents and senior leadership for crisis communication planning.

Crisis Communication Principles

To be consistent, a communication principles format is used here to form the foundation for recommendations in this critical area of leadership during turbulent times. Such a format is similar in design to the basic assumptions and guiding principles presented in previous chapters.

Principle 1: Everyone involved with communicating information to the press, district patrons, or district employees should avoid minimizing the crisis.

There are several levels to this principle. The first is the superintendent's communication with the school board. As is discussed elsewhere in this manual, the superintendent must decide whether to focus on the most current financial information only or to further investigate future predictions of revenue shortfall. In other words, is this a one-time situation or could the district face additional cuts during the upcoming year or years. An ongoing situation may provide a much bleaker picture of the overall financial crisis. This principle argues for the superintendent to present the school board with the "worst-case" scenario.

Educators are generally very positive people. For example, when speaking with parents, teachers and administrators usually err on the side of discussing how to help the student reach his potential, rather than making blunt statements about a child's low achievement, questionable behavior, or inappropriate social skills. It is laudable that educators believe every child can achieve or develop to their maximum potential. During a financial crisis, similar behavior might be to emphasize the best-case scenario. But a severe financial crisis requires a clear focus on the cold, hard facts of insufficient funds. In a word, all should be told that the district cannot continue to operate as it has been operating. The school board needs to know how bad the financial crisis is, *or might be.* When facing a real financial crisis, the superintendent should not try to sugar coat the message by presenting only the best-case scenario.

The second level of this principle addresses the full extent of the financial crisis. Both the school board and the district employees should be provided with all of the information available on this topic. A major financial crisis such as the type described in this manual will potentially affect every employee. If the economic projections indicate the financial crisis could extend over several years, it is better to get this information out in the open now, rather than delay the information and hope the projection does not come to fruition. In the final analysis, the superintendent is well advised to err on the alarming side during all steps of the communication spectrum.

When a worst-case scenario is used it provides an opportunity to reduce, if not eliminate, the number of times the school board and employees must address a financial crisis. While this communication principle may cause concern with some superintendents, each should consider one basic question: "How many times do they want to return to the school board with another budget reduction target?" The same point might be phrased for a different audience. How many times do they want to face district employees and announce more budget cuts are needed?

The communication action to inform the school board of the financial crisis should include three elements: (1) an analysis of the most immediate dollar amount that must be cut from the budget; (2) an analysis of the most probable dollar amount that should be cut from the budget; and, (3) an analysis of the worst case dollar amount that could potentially be cut from the budget. The superintendent should request the school board take official action authorizing the preparation of a budget reduction plan that addresses each of the three scenarios. School board action solidifies the direction the district will take to address the financial crisis. Further, experience has evidenced the district can achieve some stabilization when surety of direction and action is received by district employees and the community at large. And finally, when dealing with communication between the school district and community groups, legislative bodies, and the media, a school board action helps everyone clearly focus on the direction the district will take to respond to the financial crisis.

Principle 2: Reinforce the district's mission and vision statements and overall district values with employees and the community.

A critical component of the communication with employees and the community is the reinforcement of the vision and the values of the district. During a financial crisis employees will experience a variety of emotions ranging from anger to distress. The financial crisis facing the district may also be occurring in the business community and with the jobs of other family members of district employees. When the financial crisis extends from the district to the overall community, a double hit occurs on the emotions of those who work in the school district.

One example should make this point. During one economic downturn, two school district employees, a husband and wife who were both building principals in a school district, experienced a severe downturn in the property values and occupancy rates in an apartment complex where they had invested their money. Their retirement plans were to live off their retirement income and the cash flow of the apartment complex. The drastic economic downturn severely impacted their plans and each had to postpone their retirement, thus extending their working years well beyond what they had originally planned. Obviously, the stress on the "home front" compounded the stress they found on the job.

Such multiple examples of stress can occur on a frequent basis during a major financial crisis. The superintendent and senior leadership, including building principals, must recognize this possibility and plan their communication strategies accordingly. Blum (2009) identifies five keys to effective communication in a crisis that are applicable when a district faces a financial crisis. They are:

1. Clarity
2. Repetition
3. Honesty
4. Empathy
5. Efficacy (Give them something to do)

Superintendents and senior leadership must set the example for all district supervisory personnel by embracing each of these five keys to effective communication.

Clearly communicating the vision and values of the district can provide a visible message for employees to emphasize. Employees need to be reassured that the district will survive the crisis and that all options to help retain personnel are open for discussion. Further, they need to know their jobs are important to the district and the district respects their contribution to the education of the youth in the community. Repeating this message at every opportunity in a variety of settings is essential to maintaining some stability in the district. School leaders must always realize that, despite economic conditions, children are still attending school, children must still achieve, and children will still graduate. A child's life is not "put on hold" until the crisis is over; their lives continue despite the district's financial problems.

Finally, communication with employees and the community must be honest. The possibility that jobs may be affected and programs cut should be included in any communication strategy. Empathizing with employees and community about this probability should be a cornerstone of any communication. This message should be delivered with a carefully thought out approach. Selective language, tone, and presentation should be used when delivering such a threatening message. The operating rule suggested by one source is "One negative statement is equal to three positive statements" (Covello 2003). Or, as a home repairman stated to one of the authors, "It takes ten positive recommendations to off set one negative comment."

Assuring that appropriate messages are delivered does not happen by accident. A systematic approach of delivering key messages should be scheduled each workday and week. Out of the office and into the school community should be the watchword of these efforts. Numerous opportunities are available for district leadership to underscore the district vision and core values, along with communicating the need to address the financial crisis.

most? out of office (handwritten)

least: review of budget info. (handwritten)

Some examples of these opportunities mentioned above are:
- Increase the number and type of school visits;
- Have lunch with maintenance workers, bus drivers, and other support staff;
- Attend a school faculty meeting and listen to their issues;
- Schedule presentations on the financial crisis to groups of district advisory groups;
- Meet with students, especially senior high school students, and explain what is happening and the potential effect on school programs and activities;
- Arrange special sessions with building principals, on-site, to discuss the potential impact of the financial crisis on their school;
- Ride a school bus to or from school to show support for the drivers and their task;
- Serve lunch at a school cafeteria to show support of nutrition employees;
- Meet regularly with individual board members to listen to what they are hearing in the community;
- In large school districts schedule K-12 attendance area meetings open to faculty and support staff to listen to their questions and suggestions; or
- Meet with each district program advisory committee to explain the dilemma the district faces, and hear their concerns and suggestions.

Each of the out of office experiences will require time and energy. However, the benefits will more than make up for the perceived loss of time in the office. Remember, the goal is to keep the family of educators and the community working together during these tough financial times. Routine operational matters can either be delegated or delayed. Obviously, the school board should support the superintendent in allocating time for these activities.

In addition to face-to-face communication there should be opportunities for both employees and community members to review available budget information. If possible, a summary sheet, no more than one page front to back, should be prepared to provide summary budget information by program or service category. The types of information that should be included in addition to the budget figures could be, (1) the number of classroom teachers, (2) the number of building and district administrators; (3) the pupil-teacher ratio comparison with similar districts; (4) the ratio of administrators, building and district, to classroom teachers with a comparison to state or national standards; and, (5) a summary of federal, categorical funds.

Every administrator should have this information on his or her desk. These sheets can provide ready, accurate information to inquiries from within and without the district. When such information is readily available to district employees and community members the trust level is increased. Further, a checklist should be prepared that ensures all key stakeholders, including the media, are included in the communication tree for the district (see worksheet at end of this chapter). Finally, where personnel are available, a weekly "Budget Reduction Brief" should be provided to each school board member. Again, this should not exceed more than one page, front to back.

Principle 3: Engage Stakeholders in Solving the Financial Crisis.

This communication principle can provide substantial benefit to the school board and superintendent in two ways:
- (1) Provide an opportunity for the superintendent to fulfill a commitment to collaborative leadership, and,
- (2) Enable employees/community stakeholders to contribute to solving the financial crisis.

Several vehicles are available to the superintendent to achieve this communication principle. The most traditional is the school board hearing and/or school house meetings. Both methods assist in providing information on a variety of budget reduction suggestions. But there can be a possible negative. The result of such a school board hearing is usually a requirement by the superintendent to present a rationale as to why the suggestions should or should not be accepted. This only reaffirms to employees and community members the existence of a "top-down" leadership approach. In a financial crisis environment anything that detracts from the belief that a collaborative approach to solving the financial crisis can engender unnecessary negative feelings about the district leadership, including the superintendent and the school board.

The authors suggest consideration of several other methods for obtaining input that substantially reinforce the collaborative leadership principle, thus ensuring representation of all key stakeholders, and help the district communicate both work efforts and overall intentions with the employees and the public. First, the collection of such inputs helps in increasing the probability the solution to the crisis will be viewed as "We did it!" rather than "They did it to us." Second, the collection of inputs suggests a wide variety of strategies that can be used as part of the overall communication program, including:

(1) Creation of a district Budget Reduction Advisory Committee or Task Force,

(2) Create a Cost Busters program for Receiving Suggestions,

(3) Creation of a Budget Reduction Hotline,

(4) Creation of an "Ask the Superintendent" call-in TV show, if a cable public service channel is available,

(5) Creation of a media communication agenda.

Any school district facing a severe budget crisis should carefully consider the difficulties and possibilities for such communication programs. Each idea will be presented as a communication principle:

Collaborative Activity A: Create a Budget Reduction Advisory Committee.

If only one stakeholder input strategy is available, the Budget Reduction Advisory Committee (BRAC), coupled with a Cost Busters program, should be the priority. The direct involvement of key stakeholders in the review and analysis of budget reduction recommendations is extremely powerful. It serves two goals. First, this strategy supports the collaborative leadership principle. Second, the members of the committee should be asked to discuss issues with as many friends, family members, or other acquaintances as possible. It is helpful if the community as a whole can see a variety of individuals working to collect ideas, listen to arguments for or against recommendations, and then working together to finalize the ideas for presentation to the district and its board. In other words, it helps make everyone feel that they have a connection to solving the problem.

Such involvement can result in providing valuable assistance to the superintendent and school board as they address the financial crisis. In addition, advisory committee members can provide much needed testimony as to the viability of a specific recommendation. Further, when the recommended budget reduction package is presented to the school board there is a high probability the advisory committee members will testify in favor of the superintendent's recommendations. In fact, in one district with eight different bargaining groups, the total package was totally supported by those groups and the school board did not change any portion of the final recommendations.

The membership of the Budget Reduction Advisory Committee will depend on the size of the school district and the type of bargaining groups or citizens groups available. Also, participation will depend on the willingness of stakeholder representatives to participate. Central office administrators should not be members of the committee, but should be available to provide technical assistance to the committee.

A key provision for membership on the committee is the support of consensus decision-making. Members must be willing to back the group decision, once the committee reaches a decision on any specific recommendation. In addition, members must be willing to adhere to four rules:

1. To represent their constituents in the review and analysis of all budget recommendations;

2. To serve as a major communicator conduit for the group they represent;

3. To provide expert advice to other committee members regarding the potential impact an any recommendation; and,

4. To assist with an ongoing evaluation of the budget reduction process as needed.

Specific details of the consensus decision-making process will be outlined in later chapters.

Collaborative Activity B: Create a "Cost Busters" Program to Receive Suggestions.

This process will be detailed in a later chapter. Suffice it to say for now that a key component of creating an atmosphere of collaboration is to formalize a procedure for receiving budget cut suggestions from all employees, patrons, and/or community members. No one has a monopoly on good ideas; therefore, during a financial crisis, it is important to collect every possible idea for budget cuts.

The creation of a formal process for (a) receiving, (b) evaluating, and (c) rewarding suggestions is needed for several reasons. First, everyone should be encouraged to make suggestions for budget reduction. A formal process should make it easy for individuals to make suggestions and for the school district to receive suggestions.

Second, every idea must be honestly considered and evaluated, but the evaluation must be reviewed. It is too easy for a supervisor to simply say, "We've never done it that way." A budget crisis demands new ideas, new procedures, and, if necessary, new managers who are not afraid of change.

Finally, some procedure should be put into place to reward an individual making a cost buster suggestion that is put into practice. It need not be money. Recognition and appreciation may be all that is needed, especially in a time when dollars are scarce. But the basic principle never changes: Individuals appreciate recognition and reward. When setting up a cost busters program, never forget to recognize those making good suggestions.

Collaborative Activity C: Create a Budget Reduction Hotline.

This initiative should be the easiest to activate. Regardless of the size of the school district, someone can be designated to answer the "hotline" phone. This can either be an existing secretary who handles this duty in addition to other duties; or the specific assignment could be given to one secretary. Where sufficient secretarial help is not available the district might even seek out voluntary help. If insufficient phones are available the district might request a donated phone line from the local phone company. Regardless of the technique for obtaining such a hotline, some operating guidelines should be developed. A few are:

- All callers should be treated with courtesy and respect.
- There should be no discussion of the callers recommendation.
- The response to all suggestions should be: "Thank you for calling the Budget Reduction Hotline. May I have your suggestion? I will write down your recommendation and read it back to you for the purpose of accuracy."
- Then: "Thank you for your recommendation. I'll give this to the superintendent and you will receive a response to your call. May I have your contact information?"
- If the caller refuses to provide contact information they should be informed the information will be included at a regularly scheduled Board meeting, or any other such process the district decides to use.

If more than one person will be managing the Budget Reduction Hotline phone there must be some training provided to assure consistency. Finally, if possible, the phone line should be available two hours after the normal workday in the community. This will give a clear message to the community that the district is serious about receiving recommendations.

Collaborative Activity D: Create an "Ask the Superintendent" Call-in Show.

Most school districts, and certainly large districts, have available cable television links in every school. In addition, a community service channel is usually available. In some situations a special set up channel can be arranged through the local cable company. If this avenue is available the creation of a call-in show where stakeholders can speak directly to the superintendent is recommended. This is a particularly useful strategy if the financial crisis is expected to continue over an extended period of time. Experience indicates a once a month call-in show is sufficient, if adequate publicity is given as to the time, channel, and duration of the show.

Principle 4: Engage the Media in Communicating the Financial Crisis to the Public.

This principle is presented in a positive manner. Realistically, the school board, superintendent, all senior staff, and others in leadership positions will either drive the media reporting *or* the media will drive such reporting. Too many times the authors have observed a closed mentality by the school district leadership. Such "closed thinking" is characterized by limited contact with the media, holding critical information from the media in the belief that the media could not accurately report the information to the community, and responding to media inquiries with broad sweeping comments that do not effectively state the district's message.

The authors recognize the media are in the business of selling newspaper ads or TV time, and this can create a sense of unease with sharing key information with reporters. However, the media is one of the members of your communication tree that is designed to get the accurate message transmitted in order to avoid unfounded rumors and inaccurate information. Some suggestions may be helpful.

- Initiate the first contact with the media.
- Tell your story clearly, honestly, and accurately.
- Provide the media with printed materials to document your oral presentation.
- Meet first with the editorial boards of the local newspaper, radio, and television, not with a reporter. This issue is too critical to the community to leave the understanding of issues to a single reporter.
- Schedule a regular press conference with the media, with appropriate printed materials available.
- Monitor what the media reports. If the information is not accurate or slanted, challenge the reporting at the highest level of the media organization.
- Prepare senior leadership and school principals with a list of do's and don'ts for interacting with the media.
- Do not locate all communication with the media to one office. Empower your direct reports and building administrators with the freedom to speak with the press.

Effective school districts have a well thought out communication process for addressing media inquiries or reports. Even more importantly, in times of financial crises, effective school districts have a well thought out communication plan to keep everyone informed on (a) the problem, (b) efforts being made to solve the problem, and (c) final recommendations to the board that will come from the problem solving process being used.

Principle 5: Determine Who Can Speak to the Media.

It is important for the district to consider this issue. Who speaks to media probably cannot be controlled. For example, a reporter might attend any building level function and pose a seemingly innocent question to a building principal. The innocent answer could appear as a headline or as a talking head in the nightly news; the innocent question and answer might then cause difficulties for some time. The point should be obvious. If any district administrator might be asked questions by representatives of the media, then he or she should be prepared to answer the questions *on a personal basis, using the official language of the district's media plan.*

The question of who speaks for the district is vital. In small school districts the media person may, in fact, be the superintendent. However, medium to large school districts often have someone employed for this responsibility. This person, in the authors' view, should be primarily a facilitator of information to the media. Unfortunately, some press officers or public relations personnel are of the opinion that they were hired to be the sole spokesperson for the district.

In the authors' view the person responsible for media coordination, whether the superintendent or the district's public relations representative, should be adequately prepared. In addition, any district administrator speaking to the media should make his or her statements within the framework of the district's communication plan. This suggests one immediate and serious recommendation.

The effective school district has a "choir practice" program for all administrators in order to help them speak effectively to the media about the financial crisis. In other words, the leadership personnel in the district are given some training and/or recommendations for communicating with the media. For example, all comments should be made within the confines of "the process being used for recommending budget cuts." In other words, every administrator who is speaking for himself or herself should emphasize that "my word is not the final decision; we have a group of people working within a well defined process to determine the actual size and area of budget reductions." Or, any personal opinion might be phrased using the qualification of "What I personally think is important on one issue is not the ultimate concern; any budget change must be viewed in the context of comparing one suggestion to all suggestions being considered."

Principle 6: Identify Who Speaks for the District and Inform the Media of this Decision.

When considering who speaks for the district, it should be the superintendent or the superintendent's direct spokesperson. Obviously, the superintendent speaks for the district. The district's public relations specialist should be available to speak with the media on behalf of someone in a leadership position, *only if asked by that person or directed to do so by the superintendent.* And even then, the public relations specialist should remember to qualify all comments in terms of the overall budget reduction process being used.

The reason for emphasizing the process is singular: Until a final decision is made, *by the school board approving a recommendation that has come through the budget reduction process,* any and all statements are hypothetical or conditional. This condition should be continually emphasized in the choir rehearsals given to and for all district administrators or representatives who might be speaking directly to the media.

It is also important to inform the media of who delivers *official district statements* on the budget crisis. Reporters may (and will) talk with many different individuals: administrators, principals, teachers, parents, etc. But if they wish to report the school district's position, then they should know who makes all official statements for the district concerning the budget reduction process. It is important that everyone realize one fact: *Rumors will abound.* So media representatives should know precisely who to call when reporting and/or confirming statements received from any district stakeholder.

The authors recognize the aforementioned position may not be entirely acceptable to many superintendents. Nevertheless, the two basic points must be considered. First, anyone may speak to the media. It is impossible to stop reporters from reporting and people from talking. Second, it should be made clear to all media representatives that only the superintendent or the superintendent's representative speaks for the district.

But, since any district or building level administrator might speak to representatives of the media, the superintendent should recognize that leadership personnel in a district should be able to effectively communicate with the media without causing additional problems. It should be made clear to all administrators that they should continually emphasize the key points emphasized in the district's budget reduction process, the district's media plan, and provided to them in the choir rehearsals. If administrators are not capable of speaking to reporters within the guidelines set by the district, perhaps they should not be employed as district administrators.

Summary

The recommendations and examples described in this chapter are an introduction to specifics outlined in the remaining chapters. Once the reader has consumed the manual they should readily see the linkage between the need for good communication and the ideas presented in the remaining chapters.

References

Blum, Andrew. Retrieved October 14, 2009. www.wildfirelessons.net. ICONS Project, Center for International Development and Conflict Management, University of Maryland.

Covello, Vince. Retrieved August 10, 2009, www.health.gov/leadership/2006. As reported by Joyce Gaufin, April 5, 2006. Great Basis Public Health Institute, Salt Lake City, Utah.

Gaufin, Joyce. Retrieved August 10, 2009, www.health.gov/leadership/2006. Great Basis Public Health Institute, Salt Lake City, Utah.

Klann, Gene (2003). *Crisis Leadership, Using Military Lessons, Organizational Experiences, and the Power of Influence to Lesson the Impact of Chaos on the People You Lead*. Greensboro, NC: Center for Creative Leadership, p 23.

Mitroff, Ian I. (2003). *Crisis Leadership: Planning for the Unthinkable*. John Wiley and Sons, Hoboken, NJ.

Chapter 5 Worksheets

Communicating in Times of Financial Uncertainty

Leaders are listeners; to whom are you listening and what are you listening for?

Communication Sheet #1: Guidelines

Handout Stating Communication Guidelines

Making serious budget reductions is threatening. Therefore, it is important to have "guidelines for behavior" on communication, during and after committee meetings. Discussions must focus on issues, not personalities. While a committee consideration may be discussed outside the committee meetings, the information should be of a general nature and all specific budget amounts, members backing the proposal, and other details should be left out of any discussion. To ensure that meetings remain cordial, consider this basic set of ground rules as you begin.

---

1. All communications consider issues, not individuals. Avoid naming names in all situations.

2. Accept any suggestions on face value; don't look for hidden agendas.

3. Accept suggestions when offered; you then may reject any that do not meet the defined criteria.

4. Respect all comments by actively listening to the ideas presented.

5. Equality of membership is vital; equality of ideas is also vital. Everyone and everything receives the same examination.

6. Reject stereotyped positions: Examine data, not opinions.
   a. "Our school can't survive without this program."
   b. "We'll hide in our hole and wait this one out."
   c. "I have the information; I'll get back to you."
   d. "I have the money and I'll take care of you."
   e. "We'll just send a memo; I don't want to face them."
   f. "The ___ made me do that." (Fill in the name of the appropriate group or organization.)

7. Work with plain English, not technical or professional jargon.

8. Represent your true patrons (teachers and children) not special interest groups.

9. Use the "tough love" concept to disagree when needed without being disagreeable.

10. In the final analysis, everyone must accept that there are "no excuses, just solutions" when attempting to communicate.

Crisis Communication Principle 1		Agree	Plan Exists	Revise	Develop	Completed	Activited	Completion Date	Comments
I	Employees responsible for crisis communication should avoid minimizing the crisis.								
A	The school board has received communication regarding severity of the financial crisis.								
1	Most immediate needs								
2	Most probable situation								
3	Worst-case scenario								
B	School board understands crisis may worsen.								
C	School board approval authorizes superintendent to prepare and implement communication plan.								
D	All available information about severity of the crisis has been presented to school employees.								
1	Administration								
2	Professional Staff								
3	Support Staff								
E	Key community stakeholders have been informed of financial crisis severity.								
F	Local media have been informed of financial crisis severity.								

Chapter Six

Basic Axioms for the
Budget Reduction Process

This one step, choosing a goal and sticking to it, changes everything. (Reed 2009)

Chapter Assumptions: Four basic assumptions, virtually axioms, serve as foundation for this chapter.
1. Axioms, or the underlying foundation or beliefs of the budget reduction process, are stated when entering the process and are agreed upon by all.
2. Axioms are non-negotiable; once agreed upon, everyone uses them to "play by the same rules."
3. An axiom can be changed once the process begins only when there is agreement that a better way exists.
4. Axioms guide all actions by all participants. No one plays outside the rules.

Chapter Objectives: Information presented should help the superintendent:
1. Identify the major axioms underlying the budget reduction process.
2. Demonstrate that all must agree with those axioms and work together to accomplish them.
3. Provide a planning worksheet that will assist in local planning and approving of the basic axioms for a district.

Introduction

The word "axioms" is used to describe the concepts underlying the budget reduction process for a reason. Mathematicians, when working to create and define a mathematical system, begin with basic axioms. These unproven assumptions underlie the entire system; all else is proven, or stems from, these basic points. The same is true for this budget reduction process. Everyone agrees, up front, in the beginning stage, that the goals of the process, the rules for the process, and the final outcomes of the process must be determined by all players who are using the same set of rules and following the steps of the same playbook. There are no exceptions; there are no last minute changes to place someone's pet project back into the budget with no new and equal cuts recommended at the final approval stage; everything that is done goes through the same procedures. In other words, everyone plays by the rules that stem from the basic, beginning set of axioms or rules!

The budget reduction process described in this manual is designed to as a foundation for both emergency budget reductions and for long-term budget planning. Unfortunately, the continued uncertainty of public education funding implies that a process helping a district focus upon its basic job or primary tasks will be necessary for some time. While the major points outlined in this chapter are essential to an immediate financial crisis, they also serve as the cornerstones of meeting either (a) additional budget cuts or (b) determining where additional dollars should be placed if they were to be provided.

To assure the success of any budget reduction process, a clear understanding of the same set of basic axioms, or the underlying ideas that will be used to identify and assess all budget reduction suggestions, is required of all. Similarly, the acceptance of axioms is expected of all; no one plays outside the rules! The school board, the superintendent, senior leadership team members, and building principals must work together if the process is to succeed. These entering axioms reinforce the very reasons the school district exists and must serve to guide all budget reduction actions. As the process starts, it is vital that all involved accept the same basic axioms for completing the task, and also agree to use the same guiding principles while working on the task. Agreeing, at the beginning of the process, upon the basic axioms and organizing principles will enable the superintendent and school board to adapt changes and reform the basic way a school district responds to financial crises.

A Starting Point

One major point is necessary to begin this chapter. Most economic downturns or revenue loss situations do not occur in the dead of the night. Some events in the life of a school district, a natural disaster, such as fire, earthquake, or structural building collapse, are unpredictable. But almost all economic downturns are projected prior to their actual occurrence. The degree of the financial crisis, however, may not be predictable. Or, stated differently, economic booms cannot last forever. So, even in the best of times, a downturn will eventually occur.

A message should be clear: The global economy now impacts either the state or the local economy more than at any other time in our history. Prudent administrators must be prepared for financial uncertainties. This message holds true for all communities, but especially for any community with reliance on a single revenue source (oil, cattle, lumber, tourism, mining, etc.) This is true whether or not a school district is large or small, urban or rural, rich or poor. Everyone must be prepared for financial uncertainty.

The budget reduction planning process described in this manual is designed to serve as the foundation for such preparation. This process enables administrators and school board members to adapt, change, and reform the manner in which school district budget planning occurs, both now and in the future. Establishing a set of basic axioms and assumptions to enable the board and administration to work within a well-defined framework throughout the process will be given here, as well as a description of the initial school board actions required to identify and support the basic starting points.

What are the major assumptions a district should use in determining how to spend its money? The authors suggest the following, but a superintendent should feel free to add others that are basic to his or her district. One point should be emphasized when adding assumptions. Each should be valid in economic good times; each should be especially valid in difficult economic times.

Axiom 1: Schools Are for Learning and Teaching
There is an axiom in the business world that applies to all budgeting situations. The leaders of successful organizations *keep first things first*. To use a total quality management idea applied in the busi-

ness world, it makes no difference if auto company executives finish their annual reports on time if the company's product, the new car, won't start when a customer turns the ignition key. To an automobile company executive, keeping *first things first* means that the product, the automobile, must be delivered in perfect shape: clean, working properly, and ready to be driven home.

So, what is *first* for schools? How might a superintendent or school board *keep first things first?* Every school board member, every school superintendent, and every building principal should remember one thing. *Schools are about children learning.* Schools are about instruction: teachers teaching to help children learn. While this may appear to be obvious, reports of and discussions about budget reduction practices frequently ignore this basic assumption. In some instances, expediency results in core elements of the budget related to teaching and learning being sacrificed. Therefore, the authors of this manual urge administrators dealing with a financial crisis to focus on budget cuts that have a positive impact (or at least a minimum negative impact) upon the classroom.

Axiom 2: The Budget Reduction Process Must Ensure Planning for the Immediate, Most Probable, and Worst-Case Scenarios

Clearly, administrators must address the most immediate revenue shortfall. However, the overall process of budget reduction must also address potential future revenue shortfalls. Unfortunately, many efforts to reduce budgets during difficult financial times only address the most immediate shortfall. When revenue continues to decline, the school community must endure another crisis, one that could have been avoided with more detailed planning at the onset of the first budget crisis. A common pitfall, obviously, is that during each and every year of an economic downturn a new budget emergency is declared. This process, if implemented thoughtfully, will help administrators and board members to alleviate and possibly avoid this pitfall. The first year's planning efforts can guide the budget reduction process through the first *and subsequent* years.

A way of examining this type of planning is to think in terms of budget cuts in *tiers* or *levels*. Examples of this planning guide are provided on a range of possible budgets cuts from 5 percent to 10 percent and up. The terms used to describe the different situations are (a) Best-Case Scenario, (b) Most Likely Scenario, and (c) Worst Case Scenario. These general terms remain the same, even if the percentages and dollar amounts used to illustrate each differ dramatically for the local situation.

Level I: Best-Case Scenario
   Budget cuts totaling the required cuts for this year only
   A relatively small budget reduction in the 5 percent range
   A specific list of specific cuts can be made to solve the one time problem

Level II: Most Probable Scenario
   Budget cuts over two or three years, if required
   A serious budget reduction in the 10 percent range
   A specific list of additional cuts to be made if this level occurs

Level III: Worst-Case Scenario
   Permanent budget cuts impacting the district for a number of years
   A major budget reduction, in the 15 percent or up range
   A specific and lengthy list of cuts focused on the worst-case situation

While this may appear to be a draconian method, experience reveals most administrators and board members ignore facing all three of these scenarios for the following reasons:

1. It is not necessary to increase tension in the school community by planning for what *might* not happen.
2. If we plan for the highest level of budget cuts, legislative bodies will assume the schools need only these funds and will not restore cuts when budgets are stabilized and a return to previous funding levels is possible.

As a result, superintendents and school boards usually prepare for only the most immediate problem, hoping that another significant reduction will not occur. The history of economic downturns does not support this position. Recent examples of economic downturns in the 1980s, early 1990s, and most certainly the dramatic downturn in the economy in late 2007 or early 2008 all had impacts lasting for more than one year. Some experts feel the economic problems that began in 2007-2008 will continue until 2015.

Further, many states and/or local communities receive a majority of their revenue from a single source, be it oil, gas, industry, agriculture, or tourism; these government entities will always be at the mercy of volatile economic changes. Superintendents of school districts found in states or regions with such a "one crop economy" should be prepared to face changes in their economic situation or condition. They should also be prepared to face changes that occur rapidly.

Axiom 3: Everyone Will Be Involved in the Budget Reduction Process

Once a budget crisis has been identified and declared, identification of the players should be made. The authors' position is simple: When facing a crisis, everyone is involved. This means every school, every department, every service, and/or every budget category. Unless specific funding levels are required by law or mandated by the legislature, there are no exceptions. In other words, the term "everyone" was chosen with care and the implication of the term should be taken quite literally. Everyone means that every division, department, school, program, or process found in the district will participate and that everyone's budget might be cut.

One example should suffice to make this point. In a district facing major budget cuts one administrator came to a meeting where ideas for budget cuts were first being proposed and stated, "My division can make no cuts." A short discussion followed during which the individual reiterated the same position several times. The individual refused to even consider budget cuts in his/her area. The superintendent's reaction was immediate; if the budget had to be cut, the superintendent had to act. To make certain that everyone knew they would be involved, the superintendent considered three options: (a) immediately relieving the administrator of his/her duties, (b) dismissing the individual from the district's administrative staff, and/or (c) firing the individual from the school district for insubordination. The superintendent selected relieving the individual of duty during the meeting and dismissing the individual from the district in subsequent days. The point is singular: When a budget crisis occurs, *everyone* is involved. Cuts may, and probably will, occur everywhere.

The point is obvious. If a budget crisis occurs, everyone has to make cuts. But it does not follow that an "across the board cut" is the solution. Everyone makes cuts, but *everyone does not have to make the same level of cuts.* The following "critical axioms" are included to make this point.

Axiom 4: A Systems Approach Is Used When Making Budget Cuts

A key point underlying the entire budget reduction process described in this manual is that *quick fix, short-term budget reductions* will not suffice during declining or volatile revenue environments. Effective budget reduction strategies rely on a systems approach. Data should be available, collected, and reviewed in order to help determine which programs/services are the most eligible for a cut. The systems approach presented in this manual is an effective process for (a) achieving required budget reductions, and (b) building public consensus and support for those mandated reductions.

Implementing this assumes that *all budget decisions should be based upon an analysis of data*; they should not be made emotionally. Inherent in the process is the word *data*; decisions on cost-cutting measures need to be based upon hard, verifiable evidence. Achievement and performance data, along with all cost and expenditure records, should be collected by the staff member(s) responsible for such data. But it should be reviewed by everyone involved in the process of budget cutting.

A district's financial office, for example, is established for the purpose of creating and maintaining accurate financial data. The data they provide should be more accurate than information from any other source. And since the superintendent must assure that clear, factual, and verifiable information is available to everyone, he/she should obtain all data from those paid to create and collect such data. While a consultant or school patron might suggest data collection on a topic missed or overlooked by school officials, those same school officials are still best qualified to assemble and analyze the data.

Each superintendent of a district needs to determine the specific data to be collected. The detailed data needs described in this manual are only a starting point. No superintendent or school board should regard them as complete if any local situation demand the collection of additional data. The ideas presented in this manual provide a preliminary list, but each district should augment the list as required by state law, regulation, or local circumstances. The purpose for data collection and analysis should be obvious. All proposed cuts are to be backed by information, dollar figures, and impact estimates. An example of what can happen if this does not occur is best illustrated by the situation described below.

School District A

In one district, a prominent citizen who was dissatisfied with the recommended cuts from the superintendent to the school board proceeded to recommend a cut to "solve the district's problems without further delay." His recommendation was to eliminate the district's central office. If the district had in place a requirement that all proposed cuts are to be backed by information, dollar figures, and impact estimates, this "suggestion from the floor" could have been quickly rejected.

However, no such requirement was in place, so this recommendation was initially received with shock. The lack of a clear criteria, let alone pertinent data for determining the impact and the costs related to the recommended cut, resulted in substantially disrupting the meeting. The superintendent and board were required to spend an undue amount of time explaining just what the district central office did, including such things as processing and recommending personnel decisions, producing payroll checks, collecting and analyzing student achievement data, and on and on.

To summarize, as no discernible criteria or process for receiving and analyzing citizen recommendations had been developed, the savings the citizen projected had not been adequately analyzed relative to fiscal impact prior to the board receiving the recommendation. Taking any action was impossible, but the lack of an "action criteria" forced the board to discuss the recommendation.

To summarize, the creation of a "systems approach" (or "process" as described in this manual) will first guide the district in making cuts and then protect the district when unwanted and/or unnecessary suggestions are made from the floor during the board approval process. In a word, every suggestion must be moved through the system, collecting the important information (dollars cut, impact upon the district, etc.) as it goes through the step-by-step process.

Axiom 5: Each District Must Develop Its Own Data Base for Analysis

The worksheets and budget cutting processes outlined in this manual are designed around collecting school data under the assumptions stated above. First, the district should identify its own basic educational assumptions to see if they match those given above. If they do match, the worksheets provided should be an effective assessment tool to help the superintendent and school board determine their data collection needs. However, if a district identifies additional/different assumptions, then data needs may change and additional forms should be created to collect and display the information.

Axiom 6: Preliminary Strategic Planning Is Done and Implemented

Most states require local school districts to have developed a strategic plan or school/district improvement plan. If the district strategic plan is in place, if each component of the organization knows its responsibilities, and if a system is in place for continual feedback on the effectiveness of adopted initiatives, then a budget crisis will occur within a well-managed organization. The process of identifying necessary budget cuts is, therefore, highly possible.

But if a budget emergency comes before the district is prepared with this solid strategic planning base, the collection of data, including the district's strategic plan, still begins the process of planning for financial uncertainty. If no strategic plan exists, it may need to be completed. Why?

It is hard to identify proper expenditures of school money (either more or less money) if the purpose and goals of the school district are not clearly stated and if the minimum standards for the educational system are not clearly defined. The worksheets provided in this manual can be of assistance. They can be used as a framework for identifying and developing missing standards for evaluation, missing goal statements, or missing school district policy statements. Even if the district's standards, goals, or policies have been implied over the years and are well accepted, *if they have never been explicitly written and approved by the school board* possible budget reductions may be overlooked in a time of budget crisis.

Reference

Reed, Scott. Retrieved February 15, 2009 from www.DailyInspiringQuote.com.

Chapter 6 Worksheets

Basic Axioms for the Budget Reduction Process

Identify Your Basic Axioms

Basic Axioms: What are the basic assumptions from which to begin?

The manual states you should understand your basic axioms (assumptions) as you begin to make decisions. Understanding your starting point, and at the same time understanding that your axioms help guide your decision-making, is an important part of the decision-making process. Seven basic axioms are listed; your task is to examine each to see if they should be (a) used, (b) modified, or (c) omitted for your district. Use the seven axioms as the beginning point to draft the set for your district.

Basic Axioms Worksheet

	Basic Axioms	Adopt	Modify	Omit
1	Keep the classroom first			
2	A systems approach will be utilized to determine a base of pertinent information for collection and analysis in relation to:			
	Legally required			
	Required by established standards			
	Required by school board policies			
	Recommended			
3	All district departments and functions will be organized in one of three categories:			
	Direct instruction			
	Direct instructional support			
	Indirect instructional support			
4	Budget reductions will be addressed at the most immediate, the most probable, and the worst-case scenarios			
5	Each district initiative will be assessed based on the potential for achieving expected results			
6	Existing plans for pilot programs will be placed in a "holding pattern."			
	Additional District Basic Axioms	Adopt	Modify	Omit
7				
8				
9				

Num	Assumptions Guiding the Budget Reduction Process	Adopt	Modify	Omit
\multicolumn{5}{c}{**Step 1: Situational Analysis - Basic Assumptions**}				
A	**Major Assumptions**			
1	Schools Are for Learning and Teaching			
2	The Budget Reduction Process Must Ensure Planning for: (a) the Immediate, (b) the Most Probable, and (c) the Worst-Case Scenarios.			
3	Everyone Is Involved in the Process.			
B	**Critical Assumptions**			
4	A Systems Approach Should Be Used When Conducting Budget Cuts			
a	What information is available to determine which programs or initiatives are not getting expected results, thus making them eligible for budget cuts?			
b	What plans are currently being developed that should be placed on hold, thus not resulting in additional costs during the financial crisis?			
5	A Classification Sysem Should Be Used When Conducting Budget Cuts			
a	What is legally required as a result of legislative actions or court decisions			
b	What is required by established standards, whether local, state, national agencies or organizations			
c	What is referenced in local board policies based upon community desires or values			
d	What is recommended in established standards as being either desirable or beneficial			
6	Other:			

Chapter Seven

Guiding Principles for Budget Reduction Recommendations

To know what has to be done, then to do it, comprises
the whole philosophy of practical life. (Osler 2009)

Chapter Assumptions: Four basic assumptions serve as the foundation for this chapter.
1. The working principles guiding the process should be given to everyone involved.
2. The guiding principles must be used by everyone involved.
3. No one has immunity from the principles.
4. All suggested budget cuts must be in line with the principles.

Chapter Objectives: Given the assumptions stated above, the objectives for this chapter are:
1. Describe why a set of guiding principles is necessary for a budget reduction process.
2. Identify nine "guiding principles" recommended in this manual as essential to effective budget reduction.
3. Suggest required school board actions to approve and enforce the guiding principles.

Introduction

The superintendent and school board should adopt a set of *guiding principles* for the budget examination process that are made clear to all stakeholders prior to beginning the reduction process. The process that gets a school district to a new budget is important. Vitally important! The process of changing the budget is a classic example of how the journey is as important as the destination.

The guiding principles should be established and adopted by the board in a regular public meeting. A public meeting should be the forum for adoption so that everyone, those who work for the district, parents of the children who are enrolled in the district, and interested citizens (the business and political community) are aware of the requirements for participating in the budget reduction process. Everyone involved in the process needs to know the rules for changing the budget.

These principles serve as the umbrella under which everyone works. Agreeing upon the rules at the onset of the budget examination process is vital. It is impossible to achieve any form of consensus when individual players (1) all have different goals to achieve, and (2) all use different rules as they work to achieve their goals. This is why advanced planning for budget difficulties is so important. It is difficult to agree upon the guiding principles when the actual budget emergency is in process; guiding principles will impact budget reductions. But if a revenue crisis occurs sooner than expected, time should be set aside to establish the required guiding principles.

The authors have experienced extreme revenue declines and from those experiences they believe guiding principles should underlie the budget reduction process. The principles used to guide the process should be made clear to everyone, at the beginning of the process. The guiding principles are developed by the administrative staff and approved by the school board in a public meeting.

School board approval is especially important, for their approval signifies that the guiding principles are the rules to be used for guiding both (1) the actual decision making, and (2) participation in the decision-making process. Without a set of rules, any budget reduction process can become disorganized, unruly, and extremely divisive. In addition to approving the guiding principles, it must also be made clear that the board intends to abide by them, and anyone who wishes to be involved in the budget reduction process must also adhere to the same guiding principles. The school board must ensure that one set of rules applies to everyone.

Recommended Guiding Principles

The guiding principles should serve as the foundation for all budget recommendations. The authors recommend nine basic principles:

1. The First Level of Budget Reductions Is Based on the Effectiveness of Specific Programs or Services.
This principle goes directly to the heart of using a systems approach and asks the question: What programs are not achieving the desired results? Data on program effectiveness should already be available if the district has a planned program development, implementation, and evaluation process in place. The data available should be reviewed and a determination made regarding the eligibility for program cuts. This is especially true for pilot programs in their first year(s) of operation. In times of financial crisis, such programs should be continued or not continued based upon their effectiveness in meeting stated goals.

If data are not available, the district should convene a group of program implementers and determine if a specific program initiative should be retained and taken off the budget cut eligibility list. This is a sensitive area, particularly if new staff has been hired to implement the program. Nevertheless, this review must take place if the integrity of the budget reduction process is to be supported. A simple ranking process can be used to make the decision(s). Ideally, a third party would conduct the analysis, but in times of financial crisis, this is not realistic. The superintendent must ensure the evaluation process produces usable results, and the superintendent should also designate a member of his staff to lead the effort. Superintendents of small districts may need to handle this area personally or include this in the finance officer's responsibilities.

2. The Next Level of Budget Reduction Analysis Begins after Base Quality Has Been Established.
The school system must determine the minimum, base-quality education it will provide. This base quality definition should address instructional concerns, management concerns, and support service concerns. It deals with everything from "What is our maximum class size, by grade level?" to "What is the number of books that will be provided for each school's library?" to "How many administrative positions are provided for each school?" A detailed description of this process will be discussed in a later chapter.

A key point is that the district is responsible for providing a "basic education" to its students with whatever level of funding is available. Each department in a large district, and each building principal in a small district, must define what will be the educational "bottom line." The district must define what a "base quality education" will consist of. Two essential questions must either have been previously answered in a district strategic plan or determined at this stage. They are:

- What constitutes the "base quality education level" that the district is unwilling to go below?
- What are the "essential support services" required to effectively deliver a quality educational program?

Both of these areas should be part of any strategic plan adopted by the district. If, however, they are not already available, staff time must be allocated to clearly define them. While some may not see the importance of their efforts, they need only to be reminded that district patrons and staff will be raising questions about recommended reductions, and comparing different suggestions. Some comparisons and cuts can only be made if clear, rational, and defensible answers are provided. Experience with budget reduction processes clearly indicates definable standards need to be determined and readily available for the reduction process.

How are these standards determined? The educational standards for "base quality" are best determined by reviewing state standards, accrediting associations, federal mandates, and research practices that support quality instruction and include staffing and program standards by state and national associations. Decisions will need to be made regarding the level of standards the district can afford to sustain. An example would be standards from accrediting associations that typically define minimum, acceptable, and exceptional levels of service. Also, since state laws and regulations cannot be violated, a careful review of such laws and regulations is critical.

Essential support services, those outside the direct delivery of instruction, can usually be found from business and industry. An example would be standards for computer repair, custodial services, major maintenance, employee supervision, and heating or safety standards. Some standards are available from education related groups, such as architects, school bus transportation organizations, and other such associations. A careful search of available references and closely working with the business community in your area can be of great assistance. Finally, a review of community expectations is helpful, particularly if business and industry standards are not as high as the community might expect.

An example of an evaluation test or criteria for these two areas might be as follows:

- Required by established standards
- Referenced in established standards as being highly desirable
- No established standard available although highly desirable
- Not required and no standard is available or appropriate

Above all else, it is imperative to make reduction decisions based on predetermined criteria, standards, or laws. Anything short of using this approach could result in chaos.

3. *The Superintendent and School Board Will Conduct a Thorough Review of All Board Policies to Ascertain If the Policies Support the Approved "Base Quality" Definition.*

It is critical that the superintendent and school board conduct a thorough policy review for several reasons: Do the policies support the base quality educational program? Are they thorough? Are any current policies cost prohibitive when compared to the benefit derived? Are policies missing that will help guide the district during rocky financial times? It is also important to review policies before a financial crisis in order to discuss political considerations in a revenue free environment. Does a policy address issues important to many district's parents, or is the issue important to just a few individuals? Does the policy create expenditures the voters of the district will not support, even in good times, or does the policy address fundamental issues that will be supported even during financial hard times?

When it is time to suggest actual budget reductions, administrators may find that the policy review has already provided possibilities for budget reduction. Some policies may incur expenses that are not central to the district's base quality program; some policies may just not be cost effective in a tightened budget environment. It is also possible that some policies may have budget implications that have never been realized before.

Please note that this area of analysis is usually ignored during a budget crisis or when the details of budget cuts are being determined. This is a mistake. The authors' experiences over time indicate some hidden costs can usually be found in board policies. Most such hidden costs occurred when a policy was adopted for political reasons or to satisfy the needs and/or wishes of a special interest group. The very reasons for such requests are that additional money would be spent in the area of political interest or the concerns of special interest groups.

Finally, the committee conducting an evaluation of policies should include different types of district employees, including building principals and key support staff. If a policy impacts any particular group, that group should be represented by at least one member of the review committee.

4. All School Programs and Support Services Will Be Judged by Determining Impact Upon the District's Base Quality Educational Program and Support of Approved School District Policies.

Any district employee associated with a particular school program should defend the rationale for, and the benefits of, their particular school program in terms of the school district's now well-defined base quality educational efforts. If the program and/or its personnel cannot describe the program's benefits in terms of the base quality educational plan for the district, then that program has a distinct disadvantage in any budget reduction discussions. Both the program and its supporters lose credibility when they are unable to describe how the program supports the base quality efforts approved by the board. This process of precisely defining (and possibly rethinking) what the school district is about, and why all programs and/or services exist, is a necessary starting point to help address the different issues which arise during a budget crisis.

5. Budget Reduction Proposals Must Be Targeted to Real, Achievable Ends.

When the actual process of budget reduction begins, it is important that all proposals result in actual dollar savings. A budget crisis demands pointed actions, not general platitudes. Each budget reduction proposal should indicate the amount saved. This concept of real savings brings another issue to light. All too often the administrative staff is so busy trying to cut small amounts around the edges of the school budget that they fail to focus on the larger issues that might result in real savings. For example, changing policies can change costs. One of the most powerful mechanisms for budgetary change is a well thought-out modification to the policy manual. Policy changes can result in revenue reduction, and will usually result in organizational changes. These changes can result in large dollar amounts being saved.

This manual is written to assist school boards and school superintendents in those situations where real budget reductions can be achieved. An example of an unrealistic recommendation would be to eliminate all of the extra-curricular programs. This type of recommendation is usually made to scare the public into providing the funds for such programs out of their own pockets.

If the revenue decline is severe, and the community as well as the school district are experiencing financial difficulties, it is not probable the community could or would *cough up* the additional revenue. Further, if this recommendation is really not achievable, or if the amount of funds reduced from the budget is clearly insufficient, this recommendation will only serve to irritate the community. This is not to say that some portion of the extra-curricular program would not be eligible for cuts. When real budget cuts are necessary, the major point of this manual is that budget cuts should not be whimsical or political.

Each cut must be carefully analyzed, by a majority of appropriate stakeholders, in terms of its impact upon the base quality educational program definition, and approved by the school board. While cuts may be necessary in an area such as extracurricular activities, no budget reduction action should be taken before analyzing the impact of that action upon the district's base quality educational program (especially not across the board actions!). One suggestion: The use of an *impact criterion* for reviewing all proposals must be carefully monitored. If any suggestion is allowed to bypass this critical process, distrust and tension will arise within the district, *because the process will not be seen as fair.*

6. *A Budget Cut, Recommended to the Board by the Review Process, Can Be Omitted Only If Another Budget Cut of Similar Dollar Amount Is Substituted.*

This principle is absolutely essential to any success of the budget reduction process. Too often, without this principle in place, staff members, community members, and even board members find it easy to suggest eliminating a cut due to special interest group influence. However, when this principle is in place these individuals are required to thoroughly review all recommended cuts, select one to replace the recommended cuts, and convince the school board members that their recommendation will better achieve the budget reduction goal. This is not an easy task. In addition, a board member recommended cut must go through the review process just like all other recommendations. This provides an opportunity for each board member to reflect on the recommended cut prior to an action being taken.

School District A

A school board member proposed eliminating a recommended budget reduction during the first reading. The board chair asked the member if they had identified a replacement reduction equaling the dollar amount of the original recommendation. Hearing no response of a "like dollar amount reduction," the board chair gave the member two choices: (1) Submit a budget reduction recommendation to the superintendent's budget advisory committee for review; or (2) withdraw the board members recommendation as it did not meet Principle #6. Discussion with fellow board members ensued, and the recommended reduction was withdrawn.

While this principle may seem or appear to be impossible to implement, experience has demonstrated a majority of boards are seeking ways and means to avoid undue pressure from special interest groups. This principle enables individual board members to refer a recommended cut from a special interest group to the superintendent for review, utilizing the approval process, without appearing to dismiss the recommendation of the individual or group.

This principle is intended to focus the attention of the school board, the school and district staff, and the general community on a method for evaluating proposed reductions. Unless this phase is strictly adhered to, countless wasted hours will result for all stakeholders. Clearly, a systematic evaluation process, fitted to an educational environment of the individual community, must be utilized to focus all efforts on sustaining the district's plan for a base quality educational program.

Examples of evaluation points would be such items as legality, accreditation, instructional impact, etc. A further advantage of developing such a criterion is the benefit that can be derived by requiring all recommendations to meet the same evaluation system. Let's be very clear here: This evaluation process will be applied to both external and internal budget reduction suggestions. Special interest groups may find this frustrating to their cause, but responsibility and fairness are the real issues, not the self-serving needs of a given interest group.

7. *Avoid Percentage or Across the Board Cuts.*

This principle directs specific attention to those recommendations that seek to have every program take its fair share of revenue loss. Reductions of this type assume everything is equal and a specific program or service area should not be unduly impacted. However, all school programs and operations are not equal. Instruction has to be the top priority, and if an *across the board* approach is utilized, it usually detracts from this focus on instruction. Given the largest percentage of the school district budget is for instructional costs, it is conceivable that this approach would impact instructional endeavors seriously while one or more support areas would face minimal impact. The point of the budget examination process should be that each budget reduction suggestion is judged alone, and that the judgment is based upon the impact the reduction will have on the base quality educational plan of the district. The situation described below may serve to illustrate this point.

School District A, B, or C

When a recommendation was made that "simple across the board percentage cuts for everyone" would be a fair solution to the problem, the following anecdote was presented.

The story is told of an NFL head coach being asked if he treated all of his players the same? He responded by describing this situation: If a rookie were dozing in a team meeting, the coach would ask him if he wanted to stay in the NFL. If he said yes, the coach would tell him unless he kept awake in team meetings he would not remain on the team. However, if the star quarterback was dozing in the same meeting the coach might ask him if he needed a pillow. The point of this story is that all football players are not equal. One point was simply added: *All educational programs and services are not equal.*

---

8. *Key Stakeholders Will Be Involved in the Budget Reduction Process.*

This principle addresses the need to have advice and counsel from individuals and groups that have a major role in the district, or are major benefactors of district educational programs or services. This includes representatives of the various bargaining groups, parent advisory groups, building administrators, and students (primarily senior high school student counsel members).

This principle may cause considerable discussion among district leadership personnel. Some may believe they should be the primary providers of budget cut recommendations to the school board. This position will do more to alienate school district employees and district patrons than probably any one of the individual budget cuts presented to the school board. Why? Because the very groups that will be impacted can rightly perceive they have not had an opportunity to participate in the decision-making process that affects their careers, the lives of their children, or the activities of the school. The operative word for leadership in the current educational environment is *collaboration*. Of course, guidelines for participation in this process need to be diligently followed. Specific recommendations are given in later chapters for each working group or process being recommended or discussed in that chapter.

9. *A Communication Plan Will Be Developed, Designed to Keep All School District Employees and the Community At-Large Informed about Every Step in the Budget Reduction Process.*

The traditional school board hearing process, which is public, is offered to all who are interested. However, additional time and energy should be extended to employees, parents, and citizen groups who wish to have the final proposals explained. The superintendent should see this as one of his/her primary responsibilities. If the district has a school/community relations officer, that person should be charged with providing regular briefings to the media and keeping district employees informed, under the guidance of the superintendent. If no such position exists within the district, the most credible person in the district should be enlisted to assist with this communication process, again under the guidance of the superintendent. A special session with the media, once the board has received the proposal, should be held.

Schools and public libraries, as well as government offices, should be provided with the same information the board received. Individuals and groups should be offered copies of their own, for cost, at all of the aforementioned sites and/or briefings. Specific recommendations are given in later chapters.

Summary

A thorough discussion of the aforementioned principles, or other principles developed locally, must be undertaken early in any reduction process. To do otherwise will leave the decision-making process vulnerable to the pressures of the moment and subject the process to individual rating systems that may or may not benefit the education of the youth, the schools, and the community.

Reference

Osler, Sir Willliam, Retrieved February 15, 2009. www.DailyInspiringQuotes.com.

Chapter 7 Worksheets

Guiding Principles for Budget
Reduction Recommendations

If you don't have data, you don't have an opinion.

Num	Step 1: Situational Analysis - Guiding Principles			
	Principle	Adopt	Modify	Omit
1	The First Level of Budget Reductions Will Occur Based on the Effectiveness of Specific Programs or Services.			
2	The Next Level of Budget Reduction Analysis Begins after Base Quality Has Been Established.			
a	Required by established standards			
b	Referenced in established standards as being highly desirable			
c	No established standard available although highly desirable			
d	Not required and no standard is available or appropriate			
3	The Superintendent and School Board Will Conduct a Thorough Review of All Board Policies to Determine If They Support the Approved "Base Quality" Definition.			
4	All School Programs and Support Services Will Be Judged by Determining Their Impact Upon the Base Quality Educational Program of the School District and How They Support the Approved School District Policies.			
5	Budget Reduction Proposals Must Be Targeted to Real, Achievable Ends			
6	A Budget Cut Recommended to the Board Can Only Be Omitted If Another Budget Cut, of Exactly the Same Dollar Amount, Is Substituted			
7	Percentage or Across the Board Cuts Should Be Avoided			
8	Key Stakeholders Will Be Involved in the Budget Reduction Process			
9	A Communication Plan Will Be Developed Designed to Keep All School District Employees and the Community At-Large Informed about Every Step in the Budget Reduction Process			
10	Other Principles			
a				
b				
c				
d				
e				

Section Three

The Details: Plan Your Work and Work Your Plan

Chapter Eight

Step 1: Situation Analysis

You cannot escape the responsibility by evading it today. (Lincoln 2009)

Chapter Assumptions: Four basic assumptions form the basis for a situational analysis.
1. Addressing a financial crisis requires immediate, short-term, and long-term planning.
2. Initial communication requires a description of the current and future reduction possibilities.
3. A systems approach to solving the financial crisis should be employed.
4. Short-term fixes are not beneficial.

Chapter Objectives: The superintendent must define the budget situation for the board and district. He or she must:
1. Determine the extent of the financial crisis.
2. Create examples for use in cutting the budget.
3. Communicating budget reduction steps to the school board.
4. Request that the board officially start the district's process for budget reduction.

Introduction

Assessing the degree to which a financial crisis will impact a school district's budget may appear to be the easiest task to accomplish when addressing a potential budget crisis. Making this financial impact assessment is the superintendent's first task.

However, some caution should be used. Every state and locality has a legislative body that is responsible for finalizing revenue projections impacting school districts, city government, judicial officers, and other agencies responsible for sections of the state constitution. A school district's financial situation is dependent upon others, usually state government officials, and how they respond to an economic crisis. Similarly, as shown during virtually every recent period of fiscal uncertainty, national issues and events impact and/or change the financial position. The superintendent must realize that a financial crisis situation is a fluid situation. In other words, *any first assessment of financial crisis may not be the final assessment.*

A fiscal situation can get better; it can (more often) get worse. Changes may occur rapidly. The impact of a financial crisis must be examined, but school leaders must never be locked into one projection. The process for determining that a financial crisis exists and how the district reacts to the crisis must be open to change, especially those causing further revenue shortfalls.

Given the volatile nature of funding for education during a crisis, along with the normal uncertainty in economic trend predictions and state government reactions, the determination of financial crisis and discussions of it should include three scenarios:

(1) Best-case scenario;
(2) Most likely scenario; and
(3) Worst-case scenario.

In creating these three scenarios school leaders will gain understanding of the problem. One plans for the worst-case scenario, but it is helpful to know the most likely situation.

When discussing potential budget cuts, if the choice is between describing the worst-case scenario or the most immediate scenario for cuts, always begin work with the largest number. *Never project beginning budget cuts that will be less than the final figure.* Ignoring this fundamental principle is to encourage a continuous round of projections and cuts. There are serious problems associated with making rosy assumptions in a budget crisis.

By using rosy assumptions, district administrators may need to repeat the budget cutting process. If a crisis deepens and less money becomes available, a second round of cutting the budget occurs. This only increases problems in the district and in the budget cutting process. For example, a second call to make "more budget cuts" naturally implies the process may be repeated a third time. If people think *I might be back here again,* most are reluctant to consider cuts in areas or programs important to them. The logic is simple: *If I can survive this one then I still have room to negotiate next time!*

The process described in this manual is based upon avoiding repeat situations. The authors feel it is better to be the bearer of bad news *once*; no one wants to bring bad news to the district again and again. By using the worst-case scenario as the starting point, a superintendent (a) avoids bringing district staff back to make additional cuts, and (b) might even end saying, "We didn't have to make all projected cuts!" The budget reduction process should, therefore, yield a prioritized recommended list of cuts.

Finally, using the worst-case scenario as the starting point helps a superintendent respond to two completely different situations. If even more cuts are required, the budget reduction process has provided the data and recommendations to make additional cuts. If the process ended with twenty recommended cuts by using the worse-case scenario, only the first twelve recommendations might be needed. If the crisis deepens, recommendations thirteen through twenty are still on the table. Those cuts are still available. Most importantly, the process that brought the first twelve to the table is the same process that created the last eight. If more cuts are needed the superintendent and school board can use the final eight recommendations with no additional meetings, no additional work, and with no added tension. Those eight cuts were already possible; if needed, they simply move from possible to most probable. An example using a real school district with real budget problems helps to illustrate the entire process.

School District B and Its Financial Situation

School District "B" has a budget problem. The superintendent knew state allocations would be cut due to an economic downturn. After examining the final state allocation, he found the budget figures for the upcoming year were even worse than expected. More concerning was the message given to superintendents by state department officials when this year's allocations were finalized. The message was explicit: "Expect greater cuts in the next budget cycle."

School District "B" enrolls approximately 5,000 students in grades K-12. It has a kindergarten center, six elementary schools, a sixth grade center, a middle school housing grades 7 and 8, and a four-year high school. The kindergarten center and the sixth grade center utilize older buildings; elementary schools vary in age. The middle school is new, and the high school has been remodeled and expanded over the years. The district offices are located in an old school building next to the sixth grade center, and a portion of that building is used for special programs.

District B serves a city of 12,000 and the surrounding farming community. A freeway passes through the district; two larger cities are situated twenty to thirty miles away, north and south along the freeway. One neighboring city houses a university; the other houses the administrative center of a government energy site. The site's actual facilities are located in a large desert plain north of District B; the majority of the site's research and energy facilities involve nuclear power. An Indian reservation is located adjacent to and within the district's boundaries; one of the district's elementary schools is located on the reservation. However, a Bureau of Indian Affairs (BIA) tribal school exists to serve junior and senior high school students on the reservation. Some Native American students still elect to attend District B's secondary schools.

The population District B serves is relatively stable; most jobs are related to agricultural or the energy site. There are, of course, travel related employment centers, motels and fuel stations, located near freeway exits. The town's retail market situation is small, as large shopping centers are found in the cities to the north and south. The district covers a relatively large physical area; but all schools, except the school serving the reservation, are located in town or within five miles of town.

The superintendent of District B considered the problem. He obtained budget summaries for the two prior school years and the actual revenue projections for the upcoming year. He even had ballpark projections for the following year's revenue. The superintendent's overall budget information is shown in the worksheet on page 88.

The Situational Analysis: School District B

At first glance, state cuts in revenue do not appear to be significant. The district's general appropriation dropped from over $21 million to approximately $20.5 million. But as the superintendent examined the figures, he found other significant changes had been made.

First, state lottery funds, originally a separate allocation for building maintenance and construction, had been rolled into the general fund budget. A dedicated source of funds had been removed and the general fund had been reduced by the same amount. So, while legislators talked of "limiting the impact of budget reductions on school revenue," the actual results *were* severe. For the upcoming school year, District B would receive approximately $1.2 million less from the state for operating costs.

To make the long-range picture worse, districts were required to use a portion of their reserves to "reduce the negative impact" on the overall economy. The state mandated using reserves to support the "economic stimulus package" provided by the federal government. The long-range predictions were worse. State department officials warned of (a) "expecting more cuts next year" and (b) "using more of your reserves nest year." Budgets would be "tight for this year and even tighter next year!" Even using reserves, the district would have approximately $500,000 less to spend during the first year, $1.5 million less to spend the following year, and after those two years the reserve fund would be exhausted. Unless the state moved to restore funding, the budget could be down another $1 million three years out.

One other thought occurred to the superintendent. *The state budget had to be balanced at the end of the fiscal year.* In past years when tax revenues decreased during the year, holdbacks had been ordered. If that were to happen during the next school year, the district might not be allowed to spend from 2 to 5 percent of the state allotment, *and this message would not come until the district was several months into the budget year!*

Step 1: Situational Analysis: Identify Your Budget Crisis					
Revenue Sources	Budget History by Year			Budget Projections by Year	
	Completed	Completed		Actual	Projected
	Two Years Ago $ Amount	Last Year's $ Amount		Present Year $ Amount	Second Year's $ Amount
State Revenue Sources					
State Appropriation	20,199,131	21,026,299		20,466,770	19,628,431
Lottery Funds	516,255	492,706		0	0
Other State	761,733	691,244		548,563	535,135
Exempt Tax - Agricultural	61,502	53,349		35,565	23,828
Total State Revenue	21,538,621	22,263,598		21,050,898	20,187,394
Local Reserves					
End of Year Reserve Amount	1,701,340	1,500,000		700,000	100,000
Local Revenue Sources					
Reserves Applied to Budget	0	201,340		800,000	600,000
Supplemental Levy	1,975,000	1,975,000		1,975,000	1,975,000
Plant Faciility Levy	0	0		0	0
Bond Levy	869,741	796,878		796,878	796,878
Misc: (Rentals)	21,491	24,600		24,600	24,600
Earning on Investments	324,723	153,800		100,000	95,000
Other Local Taxes	80,519	0		0	0
Total Local Revenue	3,271,474	3,151,618		3,696,478	3,491,478
Federal Revenue Sources					
Impact Aid	1,076,938	501,217		635,000	620,000
Medicaid	253,857	337,380		375,000	400,000
E-Rate/Misc	303,372	196,600		220,600	220,000
Total Federal Revenue	1,634,167	1,035,197		1,230,600	1,240,000
Total Annual Budget	26,444,262	26,450,413		25,977,976	24,918,872

So the district had less money. But enrollment projections remained stable. In fact, the district was experiencing some growth. Since District B served an agricultural area and a governmental energy research site, he did not expect an enrollment decrease. No major event that might impact school enrollment, such as a factory closing, could be expected. In an era of huge oil imports, he did not expect the government to cut energy research facilities. And the farms were mostly family farms. *The district would definitely have to educate more children with fewer dollars.*

It was time to declare a financial crisis. The district faced substantial reductions in terms of actual dollars, much more than could be absorbed by simple "across the board cuts." Such a strategy might be possible in year one, but the magnitude of cuts in year two would make it impossible to use that strategy. In addition, if the entire reserve fund was gone by year three, that year's budget situation could be. . . He searched for a word. "Catastrophic" was the only one that came to mind.

Given this information, the superintendent knew he had to go to the school board and effectively communicate the problem to the district's board, employees and patrons. Planning must begin to reduce the budget. Such plans should be made for the worst-case scenario, but plans should suggest items to be restored if funds became available. The plan should indicate the order in which items would be cut.

The superintendent reasoned he needed to (a) certify that a problem exists, and (b) define the problem's scope. That was easy; he was convinced the problem existed. He would not be sounding a false alarm. He must also reach out to the community to (a) convince them of the problem and to (b) enlist their assistance in developing the solution. He must immediately resolve the upcoming year's budget situation, and he needed budget suggestions for the worst-case scenario of budget cuts in two or three years. His process should also develop a budget for the upcoming school year that included possible cuts if the state "held back" a portion of the allocated funds. That would be bad, but the worst-case scenario still involved looking at district's budget problems two or three years down the road. Year three could be especially bad. If the state did not restore the district's allocation there would be more cuts because the reserve fund was depleted.

Finally, the superintendent wanted a plan for attacking the budget problem at the systems level, one that (a) questioned each expenditure or class of expenditures, one that (b) involved representatives of all special interest groups in a process, and one that (c) was designed to find a solution to the problem. He had one final thought: A major budget crisis situation has no *simple solution*. The final plan would be composed of many little solutions, each contributing in some way, large or small, to the total plan.

Needs Analysis

The superintendent must assess the needs for the upcoming year by examining the difference between a continuation budget and the worst-case scenario budget. But other factors intrude; four other considerations must be examined. They include:

1. What are the enrollment projections for the next year?
2. What capital improvement plans impact maintenance and operations budgets?
3. What other contingencies must be considered for the upcoming budget?

In any severe budget reduction situation a major difference already exists between the continuation budget and the worst-case scenario. That is a given; that is why a superintendent turns to the budget reduction process. But other events may impact next year's budget; events that would change the budget situation regardless of any economic situation. Events under the four areas listed above will impact future budgets, events not connected to the need for reducing the budget at all.

Needs Analysis Topic 1: What are enrollment projections for the next year?

There are three possible enrollment scenarios for each succeeding year's budget situation; each has its own impact upon the budget reduction process. What happens if the district when the district faces:

1. An enrollment increase, despite decreased funding.
2. A steady enrollment picture.

3. An enrollment decrease, thus causing even more reductions.

First, the superintendent should examine how each of the three enrollment scenarios interacts with funding in the budget crisis. If district enrollment increases, the state may still freeze or actually decrease the allocation of dollars by unit. This means the district must do more with less.

The superintendent facing this first scenario will need to define the size of the enrollment increase to see its impact upon the upcoming budget. Several questions arise: Can increased enrollment be housed in the existing instructional units, usually by adding a student or two to each class or classroom. Or, will the district need to hire additional teachers? Will the negotiating unit agree to an increase in class size? If the board wishes to ask for this concession at the negotiating table, just how large will the increase in class size be? Will the negotiating unit ask for something in return? If so, what?

School District B

The superintendent of District B determined that he faced the easier portion of this first possibility. A slight increase in student enrollment was predicted, but it was small enough to be covered by existing instructional units. There might be a slight increase in class size at the elementary grades; secondary schools might need to reduce the number of elective classes, especially if they needed to add a section for a required class. But from his quick analysis, it appeared that enrollment problems could be solved within each building. If not, temporary boundary changes might solve the problem. Enrollment will not add to our budget problems, he concluded.

The second scenario is that enrollment will hold steady for the next year. This is probably the easiest situation for predicting the impact upon next year's budget. The district loses only those funding decreases set by the legislature; there are no other enrollment complications to make the situation more difficult.

The superintendent facing the third scenario must analyze what the district's financial picture will be if enrollment were to actually decrease for the upcoming year. In essence, the district will take a double hit. First, the revenue reduction planned by the legislature will have to be faced. But secondly, the revenue reduction caused by a decrease in the instructional unit funding must be added to the reduced amount of money the district will receive. The district will lose money for two reasons: the reduction of the per unit allocation, and because it has fewer units to fund.

This last scenario poses two problems for a superintendent. First, the decrease in the number of instructional units will probably reduce the number of district teachers. Will the reduction be covered by retirements and resignations? But this may be the easy problem to face. A second, more difficult question is: "What impact will this have on the district's constant or fixed costs?" Will the district have to reduce the amount of money it spends on fixed costs? What are examples of such fixed, or relatively fixed, costs? Consider the following general list of expenses that are fixed, in total or at least in part:

1. Central office expenses
2. Maintenance expenses
3. Transportation expenses
4. Debt Reduction expenses

An individual district may find it necessary to reduce costs in one or more of these areas during times of financial unrest. But the superintendent facing the scenario of losing enrollment as well as per unit funding support at the same time may have to consider cutting several items from each area of fixed costs.

Needs Analysis Topic 2: How will the budget be effected by capital improvements?

There is another key question the superintendent must ask about the upcoming budget. The district may already have capital improvement costs impacting next year's budget. He or she must ask: "What effect will the ongoing capital improvement plan have on the maintenance and operations budget?"

There are several possibilities. For example, has the district been constructing a new building? Will opening that new building increase the maintenance budget? Or, has the district been expanding an existing building? Will that expansion of an existing building or buildings have an impact on the maintenance budget? Or, must the district expand facilities for new students, such as purchasing a portable? What will the impact of that portable be on the maintenance budget? Must you pay for the electric hookup or the water hookup, or will there be moving charges? Or, to look at the operations budget, what increases will be needed in the district's purchasing budget?

Consider another set of variables in the budgeting equation. What changes will be needed in the transportation program? Must the district purchase a bus for replacement purposes, or will several need to be replaced? Will the expected increases in enrollment mean that the district needs to have more bus routes, and therefore will need to make new purchases? Or, are there changes in state or federal rules about busing, and will that impact the number of routes the district has? Or, will those changes increase the number of busses the district needs? Finally, will any changes cause increases in gas, oil, or maintenance costs for the district?

As a budget crisis is examined, the superintendent must consider previously planned increases in capital improvements. A continuation budget may have these increases built in; therefore, a reduced budget must deal with those same increases.

Needs Analysis Topic 3: What other contingencies for the reduced budget must be considered?

In any budget year there are always special contingencies to be addressed. A declining budget year is no exception. There are always special situations that apply in the state or the local area, or there are always changes in the national laws and funding formulas. As a budget problem is being examined, remember to look for all special problems or concerns that exist; "contingencies" is the word used here to summarize those special problems. Consider the following list; but remember that it is not meant to be all inclusive. Any local state or district will have its own items to consider, so ask: "What is the potential impact on a budget for each of the following, if it applies?" Then: "Is there anything else to consider?"

1. Local versus state funding: Has the state passed any "cap laws" to keep the district from increasing local funding?
2. How can I review my support services? They will need to undergo the same review as instructional or extra-curricular programs. As a result, a summary sheet showing how each support service is to be reviewed must be created, just as sheets for budgets and enrollment are needed.
3. What are the local economic conditions: If the state revenue picture is down, is the local picture down also? Is it foolish to ask voters for a levy increase?

School District B

One obvious way to cover a reduction in state allocations is to increase and pass a local levy. District B's superintendent knew this was not a possibility. The city twenty miles south of District B had already tried that approach. That district had discussed their situation in negative terms, stating that the state's potential (at that time) budget cuts would seriously impact their district. They had discussed potential cuts in athletic programs, music programs, teacher salaries, and in teacher positions. Despite such threatened cuts, that district's request for a substantial increase in their local levy had been soundly defeated. Much more to the point, the request had galvanized resistance to the local levy to the point where passage of their levy at a continuation level was threatened. *I can't be put in that situation,* District B's superintendent reasoned. *If the neighboring district, with its university population, cannot pass an increase in local levy, my district would certainly not approve such a request.*

---

4. What impacts will "household moving" have on the district? Are there job cuts in nearby school districts? Will people move into your district as they look for new jobs? In a budget crisis, "new

students may still mean no new money, or at least insufficient new money." Has part of your budget crisis come from the closure of a major industry? Will this fact cause your district to lose students? These examples are used to make one point. In declining revenue times, the district may still have large enrollment changes. How will they impact future budgets?

5. What happens if the district faces continuing contract(s) with one or more bargaining groups that all parties in the district have already agreed upon? Will this continuing contract force raises in salary and/or benefits for district employees? How will this be impacted by budget cuts?

6. At the federal level, how will the district be impacted if Congress reduces the allocation for eligible Chapter 1 students? Will the district:
   a. Provide the same level of services?
   b. Refine services to reduce costs?
   c. Drop the program?
   d. Is the program/service required by law? Is the level determined by law, regulation, or board action?
   e. If you do drop the program, will such action have local ramifications?

7. Consider a worst-case scenario dealing with special education programs. What if there is no increase in the special education formula but you know district needs will increase? What can the district do about the increase in costs with no increase in dollars? Ask such questions as: "Do we have to run each program?" "If we don't run the program will our legal fees increase as we defend ourselves against a parent lawsuit?" "Is closing the program, then, a false economy?"

8. Finally, what about the hot lunch program? If costs for federal food subsidies goes up, and you increase prices for lunch, will that lower student participation and therefore reduce revenue?

Such a list of local concerns that might impact any budget decision could be continued for several pages, but two points should be stressed:
   1. What are the special contingencies that will impact the budget next year?
   2. Will those special contingencies add to the district's budget problems?
If the superintendent identifies a budget crisis and states to everyone that a major problem exists, these special contingencies will definitely influence the financial decisions that are made.

Applying the Process: Basic Assumptions through Guiding Principles

When beginning the process to address a budget crisis, it is important to use the leadership skills, basic assumptions, guiding principles, and communication guidelines outlined in chapters 4 through 7 of this manual. If all budget reductions are to fit within the structure outlined in the basic assumptions and guiding principles, and if it is important the superintendent display the leadership principles and communication skills mentioned, then it is vital to show that from the very beginning.

In other words, the superintendent's first efforts at informing the school board, district employees, and the larger community of the crisis should illustrate or apply the basic ideas outlined in those chapters. It goes beyond "practicing what you preach"; it goes to the point of beginning with the same information, assumptions, and guiding principles; then applying all of the skills and processes at every step of the budgeting process, and reviewing the final budget suggestions using the same terms and those same ideas.

To emphasize that everything fits within the basic tenants outlined in chapters 4 through 7, consider the following suggestions that the superintendent of District B decided to use when he presented the basic budget crisis to the school board.

School District B: Informing Stakeholders of the Budget Crisis

After identifying the budget crisis, the superintendent asked one question: "Where do I begin to publicize our problem?" That answer was obvious. He had to go to the school board. But the second question was more difficult. "What do I say?" He reached a simple conclusion: *It's time to use Leadership Principle Number 1: The superintendent will develop a clear strategy for communicating the situation to all stakeholders.*

His second conclusion was also simple. *Honesty is the best, and only, policy.* That will have to be the foundation of my communication strategy, he thought. So, what do I communicate at this very first meeting. He began to list his key considerations.

Consideration 1: Show the problem is serious, and you are serious about solving it!

As the financial crisis problem is identified and being presented, one message should always accompany the crisis message. "We will solve it." A corollary message should also be clear. "We will use our budget reduction process to solve the problem."

As the problem is first being presented, some possible ideas and/or solutions might also be presented. They might include such things as:

1. We will begin the process for examining our budget. The board has already been asked to approve that process. We will be contacting individuals throughout the community to work with us on solving the problem.
2. We will work to control required budget increases in a time that necessitates budget decreases. But everyone must understand costs will go up in some areas. For example, the price of gas or diesel fuel for bus service will probably go up. If we can cut routes, we might control those costs. If not, we will pay more for gas.
3. We will focus on first cutting costs outside the instructional setting. Classroom cuts may be necessary, as classroom expenses comprise most of our expenses. Instructional cuts will come last; we are here to teach children, after all!
4. We will solicit ideas and suggestions from everyone. One thing should be clear: No one person has ownership of all the good ideas that might be used to cut a budget. Ideas and suggestions will be requested and taken from everyone.

School District B

The superintendent went on with his reasoning. The financial uncertainty we face has turned into a definite budget crisis. It's time to go to work. And the budget reduction process has been identified as what and how we will get to work. What is next? What is the next consideration?

Consideration 2: Define the Problem; Don't Destroy Morale!

Having identified the nature of the problem, the superintendent must next turn to the task of communicating the problem to others. Specific examples of possible savings should be created in order to communicate both the problem and possible solutions. But please remember: these are not the final suggestions; they are simply creative ideas thrown out to encourage others to think in the same vein.

Two important points should be made at this early time when the superintendent is reporting the anticipated revenue shortfall. First, brainstorming possible solutions at this time serves to create examples, not final products. The superintendent should make it very clear that savings will be expected in all areas and from all people. When applying one of the guiding principles to this discussion, the superintendent might state, *"We are not taking the simple way of simply asking everyone to cut their budgets 5 percent; that does not seem to be appropriate. We are brainstorming to find how maximum dollars may be saved in an area, not just minimum dollars."*

Second, it is important for the superintendent to offer examples that, if possible, do not come at the expense of jobs. If the cooperation of everyone is to be expected and achieved, the budget reduction process cannot be viewed as a witch-hunt planned to get rid of people and jobs. While cutting jobs may be necessary in the end, it is not the place to start. The superintendent must convince others that a financial problem exists and that everyone must help identify a large number of suggestions offering proposed savings. This is a difficult task. It is all too easy in the budget reduction process to give the message that "I'm here to help you, but anything you do or say may cost you your job." So while completing this early task the superintendent must outline some possible budget reduction suggestions, suggestions which imply that we can save money and keep jobs, and suggestions that imply creativity is both requested and rewarded.

School District B

   The superintendent went on. We need an example budget cut. It should not attack jobs. Maybe I should use the leadership principle about making a personal sacrifice right here in the central office. And to make it reasonably large, maybe I should suggest something that implies everyone in the central office will make a personal sacrifice. But if I do that, I have to remember to run it by everyone here first. And I must remember to suggest that we are volunteering to do this. All actual cuts must be suggested to the process, go through the budget cutting process, and emerge as a final recommendation. And another thing: I could use real dollar figures to apply the principle about budget reductions must be real and include definite monetary amounts.

Consideration 3: An example should illustrate that everyone will make some sacrifice.

   District B is physically large. As a result of the constant need for "in-district travel," the district has traditionally paid local travel expenses for any employee who must visit several schools. Supervisors, administrators, technology staff, and others who travel must work with problems where they occur, so travel funds were provided. The exact budget amounts proposed in the next year's budget were:

Central office staff travel:	$25,000
Principal travel:	15,000
Other administrator's travel:	12,000
Technology travel:	3,000
Special education supervisor's travel:	9,533
LEP supervisor's travel:	4,305
SBE travel:	5,000
Board members' travel:	15,000
Total within District Travel Expenses:	$88,838

Suggesting that everyone will make a sacrifice could include the concept of reimbursement for travel. In-district travel expenses might be paid on a "one-way basis" only. The superintendent considered that example for a moment. It seemed to be a good example of how administrators would reduce costs.

   In other words, the district would pay a principal's expenses for driving to the central office for a meeting, but not back. Using this idea the district would save $44,419 in travel expenses, and each individual making a travel reimbursement request would be paid only 50 percent of his or her request. On our salary scale, such a savings would be equal to the combined salary/benefit costs of a teacher with a bachelor's degree and a few years of experience.

   He made his conclusion. *This will be part of my first example of how administrators will work to solve the financial problem. I'll have to present it at the next administrative cabinet meeting.*

School District B

One other thing has to be mentioned, the superintendent saw. One point must be clear: Some costs are required, either by law, court decision, or board policy. So I have to make it clear that everything recommended has to work its way through the entire budget reduction process. And I should make it clear this is a two edged sword. A suggestion may be turned down because it violates state law; but an idea cannot be turned down without going through the process. Everyone must know that we want all suggestions, and that every suggestion will be considered. Nothing will be turned down because "we don't do things that way."

Consideration 3: Show the problem is complicated; simple solutions just won't work!

Several ideas are offered to show just how serious the projected budget shortfall is, and also showing why a simple mindset of "cutting across the board" just won't work.

Despite revenue shortfalls, some budget increases might be required. Emphasize these are beyond school board control, due to unusual circumstances that must be accommodated. For example: Despite the need for budget reduction, local service increases might be required by law or case law in some specific area or service. A service required by law must be provided. Or, maintenance costs may increase due to the opening of a new facility or the reopening of a renovated facility. Or, laws may have increased the minimum fund balance required for the district. Finally, the district's population may be increasing while the budget is decreasing.

The superintendent must convey all aspects of the budget crisis to all interested stakeholders. That includes communicating that "even in a budget reduction year there may be demands for increased spending." But the second half of that point must also be stressed. The superintendent must emphasize that even where increased costs appear to be demanded, they will to be examined closely. How closely? One district is on record for not opening a new building, when it was finished, due to a budget emergency. The district simply could not pay the increased costs associated with the new building, so the opening was delayed.

School District B

One thing I don't want to do, the superintendent said to himself, is to make it appear that we have already made the decisions, that we are threatening the public, or that we already want to change existing contracts with bargaining groups. For a process to work, everyone must know that it is an open process. And if we want the public to buy into this, we cannot threaten them.

For example, to simply suggest doing away with organized sports or other extra-curricular activities if we don't get more money is silly. We aren't going to get all the money we need; therefore, we need everyone to work with us. We cannot threaten anyone!

Consideration 4: Show the district will solve the problem with stakeholder assistance!

The underlying point of the superintendent's message of financial crisis should emphasize: *"We will solve this problem, we will still educate your child, and we will work together to find the solutions."* As this is the underlying theme of this manual, no other examples will be provided. The basic point is enough; one message should be emphasized. *"Together, we will solve this problem."*

But the opposite position should be identified at this time. Too many districts, when facing budget cuts, seem to threaten their stakeholders. Threats may be directed at different individuals at different times, but threats are still threats. The thoughtful superintendent must ask one question: *How many times have I heard the following?*

"If the legislature passes this bill, we may have to cut extracurricular activities."
"If the local levy doesn't pass, athletic programs will be cut."
"Which should we cut? Music or athletics?"

Such "what ifs" are not the content of this manual; instead, the authors wish to cover the question of "What do we do now?" The question here is not "What might happen?" Rather, it is "What do I do that is best for all, now that it has happened?"

Communication Planning

Finally, at this beginning stage, the superintendent must decide what to do about communication. From the moment the crisis is made public to the time the final budget is approved, communication is vital. Another chapter has emphasized planning efforts for communication; a different chapter has discussed the need for a communication plan. Those ideas will not be repeated here, but the vital point will be stated. *When the budget crisis is formally declared, the communication plan goes into high gear. When the emergency is declared, school officials must be prepared and ready to use (or implement) all of the steps of the communication plan.*

This communication strategy is vital at the beginning for one other reason. If the district really plans for the involvement of key stakeholders in the budget cutting process, then the district must be (a) able to communicate with all stakeholders, and (b) willing to communicate with stakeholders on all suggestions. Valued advice and council can be received from those who are charged with providing the education services and those who will benefit from receiving, directly or indirectly, the services provided. It goes under many names: *Shared Decision-Making, Collaborative Leadership, School Based Management, Shared Governance, Quality Circles*; but in the final analysis, it is the involvement of key stakeholders in decision-making. Also, current educational leadership practices support participation of stakeholders in all areas *of major decision-making* for school districts. Budget reduction would undoubtedly qualify as an area of major decision-making.

Therefore, it is critical that the adopted budget reduction strategy involves representatives from all stakeholders who assist the school district with planning or operational issues. It is vital that the district's plan for communicating with all interested people is ready to go into effect the moment the budget crisis is announced. It might be of concern to some that an inordinate amount of effort is going into the communication plan. A review of the situation should demonstrate that keeping the public informed of the district's ability to deliver the base quality program will not be impaired. In addition, no single activity should take precedence over the budget reduction process. Therefore, communication regarding that process must be done often, made available to all, and reactions will be gladly received and thoroughly considered. The very life of the district's effort to educate the youth of the community may be at stake.

Superintendent/Senior Leadership Action Suggestions
    (1) The superintendent identifies and presents the problem.
    (2) The superintendent and senior leadership team readies a presentation for the board that defines the problem and recommends a process to solve the problem.
    (3) The superintendent presents this information to the school board.

Required School Board Involvement, Communications, or Actions
    As the review process begins, three actions are required of the school board. They include:
    (1) *Identification of the problem*: The board must hear the superintendent's analysis and approve the concept that (a) a problem exists and (b) our previously approved process will be used to solve it. If no previously planned process exists, then the board should direct the superintendent to prepare such a plan and submit it for approval.
    (2) *Create and/or formalize a communication plan for this situation*: The board should approve using the existing communication plan or approve the plan being submitted by the superintendent.

(Note: Directing the superintendent to create such a plan is not possible, *if the crisis and the communication plan must go into effect at the same time.*)

(3) *Acceptance of the stakeholder involvement* plan: Obviously, the board must approve using a budget reduction process that attempts to involve stakeholders from the entire community. Some board members, as some administrators, will want to solve the problem by themselves. The problems of such an approach may need to be spelled out to board members by the superintendent; the same concern of "if we make all the suggestions, we take all the heat" apply to board members as well.

Reference

Lincoln, Abraham. Retrieved April 13, 2009. www.DesktopQuotes.com/responsibility.

Chapter 8 Worksheets

Situation Analysis

Identify The Problem: What Are You Really Facing?

Worksheet 1: Identify Your Budget Crisis				
Revenue Sources	Budget History by Year		Budget Projections by Year	
	2007-2008 Amount	2008-2009 Amount	2009-2010 Amount	2010-2011 Amount
State Revenue Sources				
State Appropriation				
Lottery Funds				
Local Revenue Sources				
Fund Balance (Unencumbered)				
Supplemental Levy				
Plant Facility Levy				
Bond Levy				
Misc: (Rentals)				
Federal Revenue Sources				
Other Revenue Sources				

Chapter 8

Worksheet 2: Should I Declare a Financial Crisis?

Using data from *Worksheet 1: Identify Your Budget Crisis,* consider the following:

1. Where will the dollar shortfall occur? (Ex: State cuts, levy failed, etc.)

2. During what budget year will the shortfall occur?
   a. Cuts must be made in this year's budget.
   b. Next year's budget will be cut.
   c. The shortfall will last for several years.
   d. The cuts are permanent.

3. How large will the budget shortfall be?
   a. Most immediate scenario: (The minimum amount of the cuts.)
   b. Worst-case scenario: (The maximum amount of the cuts.)
   c. Most probable scenario: (Your best estimate of the cuts.)

4. Is the shortfall large enough to be considered a financial crisis?

5. Can the budget shortfall be made up from other sources?
   a. What other sources?
   b. Is it a sound political decision to try to cover the shortfall from other sources?
   c. Could the situation get worse if I try to cover the shortfall?

6. Do I go to the school board to declare a financial crisis?
   a. Yes
   b. No

Worksheet 3: Identify Enrollment Situation				
Enrollment by Schools	Enrollment History by Year		Enrollment Projections	
	2007-2008 Enrollment	2008-2009 Enromment	2009-2010 Enrollment	2010-2011 Enrollment
High School Enrollments				
High School 1				
High School 2				
Special School 1				
Middle/Jr High School				
Middle/Junior High 1				
Middle/Junior High 2				
Middle/Junior High 3				
Special Mid/Jr High 1				
Elementary School				
Elementary School 1				
Elementary School 2				
Elementary School 3				
Elementary School 4				
Elementary School 5				
Elementary School 6				
Other Schools				

Worksheet 4: Situational Analysis Summary Record			
1 **Budget Summary**	Written	Revised	Omit
Continuation Level Budget			
Most Likely Budget Projection			
Worst Case Budget Projection			
2 **Needs Analysis: Enrollment**	Original Projection	Revised Projection	No Changes
Elementary			
Middle/Junior High School			
Senior High School			
3 **Capital Improvements: Impact on Operations and/or Maintenance Budget (List by project.)**	Increase M&O	Decrease M&O	Delay
Project 1:			
Project 2:			
4 **Budet Contingencies**			

	Worksheet 5: Existing Support Service Initiative Review				
	Service	Evaluation Achievement Data Available	Obtaining Expected Results	Not Meeting Expectations	Budget Decision: Cut, Sustain, Increase
A	Transportation				
1					
2					
B	Maintenance				
1					
2					
C	Custodial				
1					
2					
D	Lunch Program				
1					
2					
E	Technology				
1					
2					
F	Business				
1					
2					
G	School/Community Relations				
1					
2					
H	Other				
1					
2					

Chapter Nine

Step 2: Establish Strategic Direction

Anyone can steer the ship, but it takes a leader to
chart the course. (Maxwell 1998)

Chapter Assumptions: Three basic assumptions underlie actions for this portion of the process.
1. The school board must be committed to the total budget reduction process.
2. The school board must be actively engaged, with the superintendent, in the analysis phase of the reduction process.
3. The budget reduction process should not begin until the effectiveness of existing initiatives or services has been determined.

Chapter Objectives: This chapter will cover:
1. Organizing the Budget Reduction Process.
2. Analyzing School Board Policies and Administrative Regulations.
3. Establishing Strategic Direction.

Organize the Budget Reduction Process

The superintendent and school board, by this time in the process, should have formally declared a financial crisis. Leaders of change indicate that how an event or activity is organized and presented is as important as the eventual desired outcome. The strategies selected to address the financial crisis are extremely critical. The foundation has already been set with the completion of the situation analysis, the identification of major assumptions, determination of guiding principles, clearly defining the leadership and communication principles and strategies, and, the definition of base quality education and essential support services. This allows the superintendent to begin full implementation of the remaining steps in the budget reduction process.

Step 2 involves fully engaging the school board and establishing a clear strategic direction that continues to focus the district on those goals, objectives, and activities that will most directly support the instructional program. Further, the superintendent must describe to district employees and the community how budget reduction recommendations will be received, analyzed, and acted upon. It is important the superintendent emphasize the process is "bottom-up," and that employees and community members will be requested to help solve the financial crisis. Steps 3 through 6 of the budget reduction process will be detailed in succeeding chapters. This will involve the formation of a budget reduction advisory committee, a "Cost Busters" program, analysis of recommended reductions, and the manner in which budget reduction recommendations will be presented to the school board.

However, as the aforementioned structures are being established, the superintendent and senior leadership of the district must begin the process, with the school board, of analyzing those segments of the district that set strategic direction-school board policy and the district strategic or improvement plan. These areas are the foundation for district operations. Fundamental to this part of Step 2 is the determination of how the school board will be actively involved. Obviously, the board will be involved when the final set of recommended reductions are presented. Further, they will be directly involved in approving the district budget for the next school year, and budget projections for the immediate future, in this instance the next one to two years.

School Board Policy and Administrative Regulation Review:
This phase of the budget reduction process is a direct link to one of the essential leadership principles described in chapter 4: A commitment to a collaborative leadership process. Further, the third guiding principle for the budget reduction process states: The superintendent and school board will conduct a thorough review of all board policies to ascertain if they support the approved Base Quality Education Definition. These two leadership principles go to the heart of the process to ensure the instructional program is kept in the forefront of all participants as they attempt to solve the financial crisis.

The initiation of this activity for District B is dependent upon the superintendent collaborating with the school board on a strategy for the board to (1) determine those policy areas for review, and, (2) a strategy for analysis of future policy proposals that avoids, as much as possible, increasing district operational costs. In addition, the superintendent needs to work with senior leadership to review existing administrative regulations and devise a process for the fiscal impact of proposed administrative regulations. Both procedures will assist with addressing the current financial crisis and serve as a deterrent to enacting either board policy or administrative regulation that will unnecessarily create a cost burden for the district. Both procedures afford the opportunity for stakeholder involvement. The following actions are recommended for this phase of Step 2:

Action 1: The superintendent should request the school board to identify policies that can be reviewed and those that cannot be reviewed.
The focus should be on sustaining the instructional program as it currently exists or as planned for the near future. This is best achieved by (a) framing and then (b) posing policy questions, rather than requiring the board to laboriously read each board policy. Examples are:
1. Facility User Fees: Should the school board require non-school sponsored groups and organizations to pay a user fee to cover the costs for facilities they use, which are now provided at no charge?
2. Student Fees: Should the school board require junior and senior high school students who participate in after school activities such as sports, music, and drama, to pay an activity fee to cover the cost of the activity?
3. Transportation: Should the school board reduce the number of bus routes for students within the legal limit to only those which are determined necessary due to hazardous conditions?
4. School Calendar and School Starting Times: Should the school board consider establishing a four-day school week to reduce district operating costs?
5. Should the school board direct the administration to determine if changing school starting times reduces transportation costs?

6. Nutrition: Should the board direct the revision of the school lunch menus and services and/or contract for this service?

7. Instruction: Should the board direct the revision of the curriculum to reduce the number of elective courses to focus all resources on meeting the requirements of the NCLB.

These examples should serve as a starting point for any policy review to identify potential cost savings to a district.

Action 2: Once the board has identified policies that can be reviewed, deleted, or held in abeyance, administrators should determine actual cost savings if policy revisions were made.

For example, one school board determined the district was subsidizing the student nutrition program in the amount of $50,000 annually. A pertinent question needed to be answered: should the student nutrition program be self-supporting? Making the program self-supporting could mean (1) an increase in the cost for each menu item; (2) eliminating the use of plates and silverware and using paper plates and plastic utensils; (3) contracting to a private enterprise to provide this service to students, or (4) eliminating options on the menu and providing one selection only. Each of these options could have a savings to the district that would avoid the district supporting the student nutrition program with local funds.

Another example relates to student transportation. One school board had a policy that permitted the district to transport students who lived within the legal limits when requested and justified by parents in a particular school boundary. The board did not have well-defined criteria for making this available to parents. Usually, if enough pressure were applied they would ask the superintendent to take care of it. It should be noted that this happened in a district that, until the financial crisis, had sufficient local funds to pay for the majority of parental requests. Obviously, the added cost in the budget for this service was not reimbursed by the state.

The board requested that a cost analysis be conducted of the added cost to the district for this service. As a result of the added cost a change in policy occurred: The board adopted a policy that established a "hazardous transportation committee" comprised of (a) the transportation director, (b) a local traffic officer, (c) a parent from outside the zone being considered for such transportation, and (d) the building principal whose school was located in the school zone where the request was being made. Criteria were established for the committee to use in making recommendations to the superintendent and then to the board. Further, all existing routes were evaluated using the new policy and criteria, resulting in the elimination of a majority of such routes.

School District B

The superintendent knew his district was transporting some students where transportation was not required by law. When a new elementary school had been completed several years ago, the attendance zones were redrawn to assure the new school had sufficient students and nearby schools were not over-crowded. Accomplishing that goal had necessitated transporting children across busy arterial streets. For safety reasons, a policy was created to say, "All elementary students crossing major traffic thoroughfares will be transported to school."

But that need, he recognized, might now be over. Perhaps the school boundaries could be changed to those major arterial streets, thus making certain that no students in grades K-5 had to cross a major street. If so, would such boundary changes reduce his total transportation costs?

A policy change would not be needed; redrawing school attendance zones might solve the problem. It was even time to reconsider elementary school boundaries. But boundary changes were always difficult. But if he could show a reduction in transportation costs, this might be the time to create new elementary school attendance zones!

Action 3: Once a list of policies has been reviewed and considered for revision, deletion, and/or held in abeyance, the representative stakeholder input should be received to determine the impact of any proposed change.

Clearly, patron reactions to any change in district policy may be different for each change. It may be that a political hot potato does not yield adequate savings; therefore, it is silly to bring up the hot issue to the board. Remember, one of the primary principles of the six-step process is to reach budget reduction goals through a collaborative process. A superintendent might choose not to bring a policy change to that collaborative process if (a) the budget impact is not large and (b) the issue will be divisive. It is not necessary or wise to hold pitched battles over every policy raised for discussion.

One way to obtain stakeholder input is to have the proposed change on a regular board agenda. The authors do not recommend this as the primary vehicle for input. If this approach is the primary means of obtaining input it provides an opportunity for pressure groups to form and inundate the board with testimony, both positive and negative. Therefore, it is critical that the board have a method for obtaining input from the wider community that focuses on the specific policy issue, allows for input at the discussion, rather than the decision, level, and reduces the possibility for pressure groups to unduly sway the board in one direction or another. The authors suggest several options for obtaining systematic input regarding the impact of any proposed policy change that involves advisory group, employee, and community at large membership:

1. A panel of representatives from identified groups could be appointed and meet to review potential policy changes that have a cost savings for the district. The group would review the proposed change, the financial analysis, and, the projected impact. They would work with the superintendent to recommend approval of those policy changes they believe would avoid impact to the classroom and have the most cost savings to the district.

2. A panel could simply review a list of policy revisions recommended by the superintendent and, with little or no discussion, concur or object to each recommendation.

3. If time permits a survey of community members and employees could be conducted to assess the viability of potential policy revisions. A survey could be implemented for minimum cost and, in some cases, has proven to be very effective. If a local college or university is nearby a graduate student could be engaged in conducting the survey.

If a survey is done it should permit data analysis by (a) respondent groups and (b) the overall population for each policy issue under consideration. This method also provides detailed data for the board as they consider policy options. One district used this method and was able to very specifically determine the views of eight bargaining groups, each board advisory committee, and the community at large. Interestingly, when the policy issue regarding the number of district administrators was raised, it ranked fourth in the items all groups believed should be a policy change that would result in budget savings.

Regardless of the method used to obtain stakeholder input prior to board review, the key issue is including those most affected in the deliberation process. This demonstrates the superintendent and board will adhere to the "leadership and guiding principles" established prior to initiating the budget reduction process.

Coupled with the board policy review should be a procedure that analyzes the operational impact of any future policy or administrative regulation proposal. One district implemented a policy requiring specific written input from building principals and/or department heads regarding either the positive or negative impact on their area of responsibility when a policy was considered. This procedure not only provided the superintendent and school board with valuable information, it allowed more time for serious consideration of any proposed change. A worksheet at the end of this chapter provides an example of the format for collecting this type of information.

Finally, one of the superintendent's responsibilities is to help the school board members avoid undue political pressure when tough decisions have to be made. With the development of the aforementioned processes school board members can legitimately respond to individuals, special interest groups, or local or state politicians that a process is in place for analyzing a proposed policy or change in policy. This does not encourage the board to avoid difficult decisions, but offers them, as well as the community, an opportunity to step back and review the proposed policy adoption, revision, deletion with as much hard data as possible. Worksheets are provided at the end of this chapter that can serve as an initial starting point for both policy and administrative regulation review.

Analysis of the District Strategic or Improvement Plan

Recent NCLB legislation has required and/or forced most districts to create both a district strategic plan and individual school improvement plans. (This is true for District B, the midsize school district used to provide financial examples throughout this text.) Usually these plans are for more than one year.

When a financial crisis occurs a district should review and rethink the goals, objectives, and timing of specific activities identified in these plans. While it may be required to continue implementation of specific plans, it is also probable that other areas of the district may have to provide an unusually large share of the budget reductions if such plans are to continue. Unfortunately, the U.S. Congress has not found it necessary to reduce, eliminate, or delay any elements of the NCLB requirements. This places a substantial burden on state departments of education and eventually local school districts to continue to fund activities that are required by the NCLB legislation. As a result, the superintendent of District "B" should ask several questions of the staff, examples of which are provided below:

1. What improvement priorities can be undertaken without new funds or staff?
2. What improvement plans can be delayed without violating state laws and/or regulation; or, which can be delayed without severely damaging the plan?
3. If additional funds and/or staff are required, can they be obtained by reduction or elimination of services in another area?
4. What portions of the district strategic plan or school improvement plans must be completely set aside or at least delayed for one or more years?

One district utilizing the budget reduction process conducted a complete review of the administrative procedures for class size and determined that a reduction of students in high school English classes could be accomplished with budget cuts in elective courses. The district also decided to reduce class size in the primary grades, and give authority to elementary building principals to initiate job sharing, resulting in the reduction of fringe benefit costs while still employing the teachers to continue an effective instructional program.

These actions require a substantial rethinking of the need and cost of numerous activities or initiatives. Considerable involvement of staff and stakeholders is necessary before final decisions are made. A financial crisis must cause administrators to look closely at priorities and administrative regulations. The district's strategic plan and individual school improvement plans provide a vehicle for in-depth analysis of district commitments, either proposed or operating.

During any budget analysis specific steps should be taken to assess the effectiveness of existing programs, particularly when funds or staff have been budgeted for their implementation. The Guiding Principle outlined in chapter 7 is the foundation of this analysis: *The First Level of Budget Reductions Will Occur Based on the Effectiveness of Specific Programs or Services.*

This analysis should clearly focus upon the relationship of the initiative to improved student achievement. Further, each planned initiative should be reviewed in relation to the probability of improving student achievement. This is particularly crucial as a result of the NCLB legislation. However, regardless of the NCLB requirements, criteria for evaluating either districtwide or school level improvement plans (current or projected) will assist the school board and superintendent in making all financial decisions.

Examples of some questions that need to be addressed are provided:

1. Which instructional initiatives are fully implemented, achieving the desired results in student achievement, and should be continued?
2. Which instructional initiatives are not fully implemented, with limited data regarding the impact on improved student achievement, but should be continued, possibly with limited funding?
3. Which instructional initiatives have been fully implemented, but are not achieving desired results in student achievement, and should be discontinued?
4. What instructional initiatives are in the district's strategic plan that might be delayed unless external funding is available?

While additional questions could be posed, these four serve as a foundation for the analysis of both the district strategic plan and school improvement plans. Question 1 covers cutting a program or service that would have a negative impact on student achievement. Answers to the other questions might enable the district to redirect budgeted program funds or cut all funding. The important point of this exercise is to analyze data regarding district or school improvement plans to determine if the funds expended, and/or the staff allocated, should be continued. Or should the program be eligible for budget reduction.

Medium to large school districts have assessment and evaluation staff to collect the data necessary for decision-making. If the district does not have such staff, a meeting with the participants in a program could be held to discuss the viability of their program or activity. While some may overestimate the positive impact of their program or service, others will honestly discuss positive and negative aspects of the program.

If the staff is requested to describe, *with as much hard data as possible*, whether or not the program or service is helping improve student achievement, and they are required to substantiate their responses with examples when possible, the superintendent can reasonably make a judgment on the program or service. Sometimes sound judgment based on experience is all that can be expected in a crisis environment. It is not essential that a superintendent wait for all data to be collected; sometimes it's necessary to make a decision based on the "best available" information. Leaders understand this point.

Examples could be provided for any elementary, middle/junior, or senior high school; District B's items should serve to begin the discussion using the four key questions noted earlier. The point is basic: appropriate district staff should review each strategic goal to determine if funding should be continued; each school should be held accountable for doing the same. A financial crisis requires rethinking of district priorities and school improvement initiatives. Establishing strategic direction in times of financial crisis is paramount if district employees and the community are to understand priorities used to determine that which will be sustained and that which will be eliminated or delayed. When decisions are made, whether supported by employees and community members or not, having people who understand the priorities adds a degree of stability as the unknown of "cut or do not cut" decision is determined.

School District B: Strategic Plan or School Improvement Plan Goals

The superintendent's review of the district's Strategic Improvement Goals indicated several specific items he could recommend to the budget reduction advisory committee for budget reduction consideration.

District Strategic Goals:

1. Increase technology tools and types available	$228,126
2. Expand communication for each school	$10,000
3. Expand the district wellness program	$23,200
4. K-12 teacher in-service: strategies to improve student achievement	$83,920
5. Increase the number/type of student assessment instruments	$107,220
6. Enhance the district salary schedule to pay for advanced degrees	TBD

High School Improvement Goals:

7. In-service on positive student behaviors	$7,856
8. Gifted-talented advanced opportunities in-service	$4,000

Goals 1, 2 and 3, he thought, are excellent examples of how we do not expand or create program costs this year. We replace technology where needed, not increase our purchases. Individual schools will have to develop communication plans with no costs. The district wellness plan will definitely not be expanded this year! He went on. Goal 6 is moot this year; there will be no raises. So that leaves the in-service plans. I've already used that example: All in-service will be done within the district; we emphasize success by having teachers help each other.

But Goal 5 is important. If we are to avoid Average Yearly Progress (AYP) problems under the NCLB legislation, we need to provide teachers with more feedback on student achievement. I'll probably have to suggest that we narrow the assessment purchases to focus on subject areas with achievement problems, or purchase fewer such assessment devices to use in schools with AYP problems on an experimental basis. If an assessment tool is really helpful, we can widen its use next year.

The superintendent concluded: I have some examples to use in my opening statements. These should suggest to each school or districtwide committee just how hard we need to look at each budget line. Some things just won't be continued using a "business as is" policy.

The worksheets provided are intended to assist the superintendent with the following actions:
1. Actively engaging the school board in the budget reduction process through a careful review of existing board policies that may have a fiscal impact.
2. Development of a policy/administrative regulation impact analysis process.
3. Identify the populations that should be surveyed if a survey of stakeholder views is considered.
4. Examples of survey questions that can be included if a survey is conducted.
5. Establishing documentation of decisions regarding program or service initiatives.

Each of the actions outlined in this chapter for establishing strategic direction will serve as the cornerstone for securing budget reduction recommendations from district employees and community members. But a process for examining each budget reduction recommendation and determining the value of each is based upon the idea that recommendations exist. Step 3 of the recommended budget reduction process will specifically focus on the generation of ideas, a process for encouraging ideas, and making certain that all proposed ideas actually make it to the evaluation process.

Reference

Maxwell, John (1998). *The 21 Irrefutable Laws of Leadership: Follow Them and People Will Follow You*. Nashville, TN. Thomas Nelson Publishers, Inc., p. 39.

Chapter 9 Worksheets

Establish Strategic Direction

Where do you really want to go?

Policy and Procedural Analysis Worksheet 1:

The following questions are provided to serve as a beginning point for the superintendent when working with the board and senior leadership team for use in analyzing school board policies and administrative procedures for possible cost savings. The list is presented as a beginning point; the superintendent should add his or her own questions to this list.

1. What policies has the school board indicated as "not to be reviewed?"

2. Which policies has the school board indicated as "open to be reviewed?"

3. Who will be involved in the policy review?
   a. Will one team review all policies?
   b. Will different teams be created to review subsets of the entire manual?

4. What administrative regulations are "not to be reviewed?"

5. Which administrative regulations are "open to be reviewed?"

6. Who will be involved in the review of administrative regulations?
   a. Will one team review all policies?
   b. Will different teams be created to review subsets of the entire manual?

7. What will the review entail?
   a. If there is a potential change in policy/regulation, does it save money?
   b. If so, how much?
   c. Does the policy change impact efforts to improve student achievement?

8. What methods should be used to acquire stakeholder information.
   a. Survey
   b. Use of existing committees
   c. Establish a special committee of "representative stakeholders."

Board Policy Issue	Board Identified	Impact Analysis Complete	Cost Benefit Analysis Complete	Stakeholder Review	Board Decision	Cost Savings
Facility User Fees: Should the school board require non-school sponsored groups and organizations to pay a user fee to for facilities they use?						
Student Fees: Should the school board require an activity fee for secondary students in extra-curricular activities?						
Transportation: Should the district reduce bus routes inside legal limits to those necessary due to hazardous conditions?						
School Calendar: Should the district consider a four-day school week?						
School Starting Times: Should the district modify starting times to reduce transportation costs?						
Nutrition: Should the board revise lunch menus and/or contract for this service?						
Instruction: Should the board reduce under-enrolled elective courses to focus resources on meeting requirements of NCLB.						
Summer School: Should the district consider eliminating summer school? For all? Limited to NCLB needs only?						
Program Reductions: Should the district reduce or eliminate progam options, such as DECA, FFA, etc.						
Other:						

Proposed Policy or Administrative Regulation Review

The policy and or administrative regulation described here is currently being considered by the school superintendent/school board for adoption. Please review this document, in terms of what you believe would be the positive/negative impact upon the department or school you administer. Please return the completed form to the identified central office administrator within five working days. Thank you in advance for your assistance.

Proposal: Policy Proposal _____   Administrative Regulation _____

(Insert policy statement or administrative regulation here.)

Potential Benefit:

Potential Negative Impact:

_____   _____   _____
Signature   Date   School/Department

Stakeholder Survey Worksheet 1

> Survey Suggestions: Conducting a survey to analyze the policy issues the school board should address requires:
>
> 1. Defining the purpose of the survey.
> 2. Determining the population(s) that data should be collected from.
> 3. Determining the size of the sample you wish to survey.
> 4. Determining the topics to be covered and the individual questions to be asked.
> 5. Determining the survey method: telephone, mail, interview, focus group, etc.
> 6. Determining the procedures for data analysis.

It is impossible to provide one survey form that all districts might use. Therefore, consider the following questions to determine (a) if you need to do a survey, and (b) what should the survey cover.

1. What are the reasons why you would (or would not) conduct a survey?

2. What populations within your school district should be surveyed?

Students?	What grade levels?
Teachers?	Which grade levels? Which subject areas? Does length of service make a difference in knowledge?
Administrators?	How many? All categories? Building and grade levels?
Bargaining Groups:	Which other groups? (Support staff, custodial, etc.) Other non-bargaining groups?
Parents?	How many? Ethnic/Gender representation? Attendance area distribution? Parents of children in each grade level?
Community Stakeholders?	Non-parents? Business groups? How many? By business category? By socio-demographic category?

Stakeholder Survey Worksheet 2

Survey Content Suggestions

    To provide meaningful data to the school board, the content of the survey should be carefully planned. The following worksheet is provided to offer suggestions on planning or creating the survey instrument:

It is impossible to provide one survey form that all districts might use. Therefore, consider the following questions to determine (a) if you need to do a survey, and (b) what should the survey cover.

Exercise One: Assume a survey is to be conducted and the population has been selected. List four or five general areas that you would like to cover in the survey:

    Example: Policies covering: Transportation services
                                       Special needs populations
                                       Administrative personnel ratios
                                       Pupil teacher rations

Exercise Two: Select one area. Write four or five questions that provide information on the preferences, by group, on the acceptance or non-acceptance of a policy change. An example:

    Topic: Policies Dealing with Student Nutrition or Service

    Fact: District B currently subsidizes the food service program; amount = $____.

    Questions: Should district increase the price of meals?

    Note: Questions must be phrased to include one and only one concept.

Exercise Three: Evaluating the responses to the questions and population:

All items should be evaluated by responses and response groups:

	Support	Do Not Support	No Opinion
Students			
Teachers			
Administrators			
Parents			
Community Members			

		Evaluation	Achievement Data Available	Obtaining Expected Results	Not Meeting Expectations	Budget Decision: Cut, Sustain, Increase
Worksheet 3: Existing Program Initiative Review						
Level	**Program**					
A	**Elementary Grades**					
1	NCLB Reading Tutoring Program					
2						
3						
B	**Middle Grades**					
1	Math Initiative					
2						
C	**Senior High School Grades**					
1	Block Scheduling					
2	Trimester					
3						
D	**District Initiatives**					
1	Professional Development Activity					
2						
3						
E	**Other**					
1						
2						
3						

Worksheet 4: Existing Support Service Initiative Review					
	Service	Meeting Expectations	Modify Service System	Requied by Law	Exceeding Legal Requirements
A	Transportation				
1					
2					
B	Maintenance				
1					
2					
C	Custodial				
1					
2					
D	Lunch Program				
1					
2					
E	Technology				
1					
2					
F	Business				
1					
2					
G	School/Community Relations				
1					
2					
H	Other				
1					
2					

Chapter Ten

Step 3: Idea Generation

It is the responsibility for leadership to provide opportunity,
and the responsibility of individuals to contribute. (Pollard 2009)

Chapter Assumptions: The assumptions used in this chapter include:
1. Those who do the work of the district, or are beneficiaries of district services should be engaged in the budget reduction process.
2. Involvement in the budget reduction process should not be happenstance, or as a respondent to predetermined actions.

Chapter Objectives: The following objectives are used in this chapter.
1. Setting the stage for reduction recommendations.
2. Develop, initiate, and promote a "Cost Busters" program.
3. Examples of "Cost Busters" recommendations.

Setting the Stage for Generating Budget Reduction Suggestions

This chapter's major concept is found in the following adage: "Budget reduction suggestions are better by the pound." The more suggestions generated for either (a) cutting costs or (b) increasing revenue, the greater the possibility that the budget reduction goals can be achieved using creative ideas rather than "across the board" cuts.

Throughout this manual the authors have emphasized the need to actively, and meaningfully, involve those who will be the most affected by targeted budget reductions. If consensus decision-making is to be achieved, all stakeholders must have opportunities to contribute. The authors experience in leading organizations indicates that employees want or desire to work together effectively, want to connect to the organization's large purpose, and they expect the leadership of an organization to provide them with opportunities to achieve personal, professional, and organization success. The same philosophy holds true for people outside the organization who serve on advisory groups. Receptiveness to stakeholder suggestions must resonate throughout the district and community.

The foundation for involving stakeholders in the budget reduction process is embodied in the leadership and communication principles, assumptions, and guiding principles described in earlier chapters of this manual. Four specific principles serve as the basis for achieving the objectives of this chapter.
1. Committing to a collaborative leadership process;
2. Engaging stakeholders in solving the financial crisis;

3. Giving everyone a voice in the process; and

4. Involving key stakeholders in the entire budget reduction process.

The emphasis on stakeholder involvement as an introduction to this chapter is intended to reinforce the belief and experience of the authors whose success with the aforementioned principles has led to effective budget reductions in several districts. Further, the extensive involvement of stakeholders in policy and regulation review described in chapter 9 highlights the importance of stakeholder participation in the budget reduction process.

The superintendent must make it very clear to all stakeholders that the district is serious about their involvement. Superintendent communication should emphasize the budget reduction process as a "bottom-up" activity. The following examples for school athletic programs are provided to demonstrate the value of a "bottom-up" approach. Each of the examples either was suggested (and failed) or was suggested, approved, and is still being used in the school district today.

Example 1: School District A and Limiting High School Athletic Activities

School administrators in District B threatened to "dramatically cut" high school athletic programs if the district's supplemental levy was not approved. This approach had worked once before for the district. However, as the district's financial crisis simply mirrored the community's financial situation, the levy was defeated firmly and dramatically.

For school District B, threatening the athletic program did not work to help the district pass the supplemental levy in any way. Rather, the animosity generated by a "top-down suggestion" threatened the district's second attempt to pass a much smaller supplemental levy.

Example 2: School District B and Limiting High School Athletic Activities

When budgets were tight in an urban area, stakeholders interested in the athletic programs came up with an interesting suggestion for limiting athletic expenses. They suggested the three urban and suburban school districts, each with multiple high schools, should limit athletic competition to their immediate area. The committee suggested limiting competition to the three districts by spelling out specific travel mileage limits. The only exceptions to the mileage limits were for travel to state playoff and championship competitions. Since the three districts housed ten high schools, they could effectively create a "round robin schedule" of nine football games and eighteen basketball games within the stated mile limit.

Since this suggestion came from stakeholders, it was accepted and approved by all the three school boards, immediately and without opposition. Further savings were obtained when the districts eliminated district supported travel to away games for bands, pep clubs, cheerleaders, and other groups. Parents with students in these groups agreed to provide their own transportation, since no game involved traveling more than twenty miles within the greater urban area. It should also be noted that the actions of these three districts did not help other districts with high schools in the same size or level classification. Some of these other high schools had to find new opponents to fill out their schedules, usually requiring more travel.

Example 3: School Districts B and C and Limiting High School Activities

Stakeholder groups in smaller high schools made and passed similar suggestions to those from Example 2. Since districts of smaller size usually have only one or two high schools they are able to limit competition to other schools in their district. But stakeholders in these districts suggested a policy of no contests out of league play or outside a set mileage limit. This policy did cost schools one or two scheduled games per sport, usually one football game and two or more basketball games. But the suggestion of limiting athletic contests to league games only came from athletic program stakeholders as a way of (a) continuing athletics while (b) reducing costs. The suggestion was passed in every league school district. The districts involved also reduced the expenses of school sponsored band travel by limiting the number of away games each band could attend. This policy allowed the home band to create and perfect longer halftime shows, as only one band performed at halftime for most games. Stakeholders in the music program approved the concept giving each band more time to perform during a game and allowing them to create fewer new performances. In a word, music directors preferred perfecting five long performances over quickly preparing ten short performances.

One superintendent commented that cost savings for transporting the football team, band, pep groups, and cheerleaders were over $1,000 less per game using the ideas generated by the stakeholder groups for nearby schools. Slightly larger savings were obtained for games requiring greater travel distances. She also said high school teachers appreciated the fact that fewer students were out of class on Friday afternoons.

Example 4: School Districts A, B and C: Limiting Athletic Program

Stakeholders in one large district decided that keeping a variety of high school athletic programs was more important than having competitive programs at the junior high school or middle school level. They suggested returning all junior high or middle school athletic activities to the intramural level. There would be no competition between schools at that level, no formal cheerleading programs, and specific to one sport, no tackle football programs. In other words, they eliminated a high cost program, competition between schools, and eliminated such support programs as cheerleading, pep clubs, and music groups. The rationale was "to include everyone in the various athletic intramural programs, not to sponsor exclusionary team sport programs at the middle school or junior high school level."

In all of these latter examples, the suggestions were approved by the school board and supported by stakeholder groups *because the suggestions came from the stakeholders themselves.* When stakeholders were allowed to examine all the possibilities, to see all possible budget savings, and to see the actual costs of all programs, they suggested ways to "save high school athletics while reducing costs," and then supported those recommendations before the school board.

The superintendent must *initiate* implementation of specific processes to ensure stakeholder input, *describe* how all input will be reviewed, and, *specify* how their suggestions will gain final approval. If stakeholders are asked to participate, they must know their participation will be valued and used. Further, it is essential the school board collaborate with the superintendent with implementation of plans for stakeholder input, and encourage employees and community members to participate whenever and wherever a board member attends a meeting, visits a school or department, and, especially when addressing the media. The overall message must be: *The district not only expects everyone to assume responsibility for helping to solve the financial crisis, but also expects suggestions from all stakeholders about ideas that may contribute to reducing the budget in a manner that least affects the classroom.* Two levels of stakeholder involvement will be provided in this chapter: (1) stakeholder involvement through actions with bargaining units, advisory groups, or other interested groups; and, (2) individual involvement and suggestions through a district "cost busters" program.

Bargaining Unit and Employee Association Involvement

A critical component of stakeholder input is to ensure that in states where bargaining is permitted each bargaining group is not only involved in the discussion about stakeholder input but is also committed to supporting the process. If possible, a written statement or resolution from each bargaining group outlining support and collaboration with the superintendent and the school board is desired. In those states where some employee categories are not permitted to bargain, they usually form employee associations. Representatives from these associations should also be included in both the discussion and initiation of the stakeholder input process. To ignore such groups can result in groups forming their own budget reduction agenda, acting outside the district process. This can, and in some instances has, created substantial problems for both the school board and superintendent. Obviously, relationships formed with leaders of bargaining groups and employee associations, prior to any financial crisis, is beneficial to both (a) creating a partnership in the budget reduction process and (b) gaining support for final budget proposals.

One superintendent, appointed to the position after a prolonged teacher strike, immediately began to build positive relationships with the teacher bargaining unit upon assuming the job. This involved such activities as (a) meeting on a monthly basis with the head of the teachers' bargaining unit to discuss non-bargaining issues and (b) encouraging the school board to host a dinner with the bargaining group leaders once each semester. The goal was to develop an open communication environment. Including the head of the bargaining unit in such activities as new employee orientation and teacher recognition events also helped foster an open environment. Finally, specific meetings where the superintendent responded directly to employee questions and concerns further promoted both trust and confidence on the part of all individuals. Similar activities were undertaken with all employee associations.

So when the financial crisis occurred the first individuals, other than the school board, informed of the crisis were the leaders of each employee bargaining group. Once the budget reduction structure was developed at least one representative (and often more) from each bargaining unit and employee professional association were included on committees that offered and/or evaluated recommended budget reductions. Suffice it to say that if little or no personal interaction with employee group leaders had been established prior to the financial crisis, obtaining participation in the budget reduction process would have been difficult.

When faced with severe budget cuts, virtually every bargaining group or professional association was most willing to give suggestions for possible cuts, revenue expansion, or savings made by delaying implementation of programs. Consider how special educational interests (parents, teachers, and the teacher bargaining group) suggested possibilities for budget cuts in the following example.

School Districts A and B

One district, whose special education program went far beyond the level required by state regulations, was able to generate savings by reducing the level by which they exceeded state minimums. They did not cut all the way back to the required minimum level program. Given the fact that the down economy was projected to last more than one year, the interested parties suggested the district create a data base with all IEP's to determine similar needs and cost efficient ways to meet those needs.

Notice the interested special education groups suggested different types of ideas:
1. Eliminating programs or services not required by law or court order.
2. Refining program services to meet law or case law decisions.
3. Recommending a centralized database to create clerical savings.

Examples of group recommendations that resulted in substantial reductions include two parts:

1. Giving a *Suggestion:* In one district the teacher's bargaining unit recommended a willingness to "freeze" existing salaries, thus resulting in no movement on the salary schedule for acquiring degrees, years of experience, etc.

2. Proving an *Illustration:* District B expects to increase its budget approximately $200,000 every year due simply to movement on the salary scale. The majority of teachers move down a step; many move over a column. The savings generated by "freezing each teacher's position on the scale" can be sizeable.

3. Giving a *Suggestion:* The teacher's bargaining group suggested that, to save full time jobs, the district should eliminate expenditures for substitutes. The teachers agreed to assume substitute duties during their planning periods, if teachers with special duties were kept on staff, those teachers would fulfill substitute responsibilities.

4. Proving an *Illustration:* If this were to take place in school District B the savings to the district would be, at least, $212,253. (A large district adopted this suggestion and saved over one million dollars a year in substitute costs while saving full time teaching positions.)

Administrative Personnel Involvement

Administrators, at either the district or building level, should be treated as a separate entity when soliciting group budget reduction recommendations. Regardless of district size, there are key district personnel who have a unique perspective of the big picture in the district. Also, building principals are particularly positioned to identify specific reductions that would not inordinately impact the classroom, while also being able to evaluate recommendations by others regarding potential building level budget cuts. Even in very small districts the elementary, middle/junior high, and high school principals could meet and discuss potential budget reductions they perceived would not hamper the instructional program. In larger districts representatives should be selected from each administrative level to prepare a set of potential reductions.

School Districts A, B, or C

All school districts should consider reducing the number of scheduled days and or hours to the minimum allowed by state law or school board regulation. Such action should save operational costs in the following areas:

  a. Transportation costs.
  b. Energy costs.
  c. Salaries and fringe benefit costs for all personnel.

This same principle may hold true in other areas. Wherever the district exceeds state or other mandated requirements, reducing efforts to the mandated or legally required level may result in cost savings.

This special emphasis upon administrative suggestions is due to the knowledge these individuals have on the budgets they manage. They often have more information than other personnel. But one department or school should not be allowed to recommend reductions that might negatively impact other departments or schools. Therefore, all administrators (or in large districts, a subcommittee of all administrators) need to review all recommendations. An example: If one high school decided to cut an academic elective, which enrolled students from other schools, this decision would impact the curriculum offerings in other schools. The review process, then, should include administrators from other schools.

School District B

   For example, purchase of new equipment should be closely examined while in "budget reduction" situations. Some may be required; only the supervising administrator would know that some type of legal or required situation made the purchase necessary. District administrators identified planned purchases in the original budget; each would have to be reviewed by (a) the supervising administrator and then (b) the budget reduction committee. Some examples of potential savings in school District B were:

Equipment replacement or repair	$45,043
Technology replacement or repair	$108,411
Alternative middle school equipment	$23,965
Activities equipment	$15,000
Administrative development	$23,000
Business office equipment	$23,000

When administrators have identified reductions they believe are achievable, they should rank order them using a code such as "high priority," "medium priority," or "low priority." Upon completing the ranking, it should be presented to all administrative personnel for input. The finance office should then compute the actual savings for each area recommended, as shown in the box above. Finally, the complete list must be analyzed using the "descriptor codes" described in chapter 11.

Advisory Group Participation

   Again, to reach a consensus on proposed budget reductions, it is necessary to have citizen or program advisory groups meet first as a special group and then as combined representatives of all these groups, following the same organizational scheme as administrators. The following questions or considerations are important.

1. What advisory or program groups might exist? These groups might include the special education, vocational education, or federally funded program advisory groups.
2. Why should these groups meet individually first? All participants in the district should have the opportunity to contribute to the budget reduction process. There are no exceptions. Therefore, the individuals in an advisory group should ask such questions as:
   "How can we make cuts in our area or areas?"
   "How can we realign priorities?"
   "How can we become more efficient or effective?"
3. Why should all advisory groups then elect representatives to meet as a group representing all special interests? These individuals must also begin to look at the overall picture, not just their special needs area. These individuals will not look at the larger picture unless a procedure is set up which encourages them to do so. It is also important for each group to recognize that if they only meet individually, then the needs of one group are pitted against the needs of another group. If they meet jointly, and come up with a joint set of recommendations, then they are in charge of their destiny, rather than an outside individual or group.
4. Once the advisory groups are together they should consider their recommendations in the same manner as administrators by using the descriptor codes provided in chapter 11. One item might be worth noting. Many of the recommendations of these groups will already have been identified; regardless, these committees should be utilized. But if the groups are not asked for recommendations, then the system will seem to be closed and support for the budget reduction process will be diminished. Further, if these groups make similar recommendations as other groups, they should still be given recognition for their efforts and ideas.

Individual Involvement: Develop and Implement a "Cost Buster" Program

Involving employees in the budget reduction process through their bargaining representatives is one clear method of obtaining cooperation with a difficult task. However, an even more direct method, that has several features discussed in the literature on empowerment, has provided considerable operational savings and enhanced the overall collaborative efforts of the district on budget reduction. The process is known as the "Cost Buster" program. The Cost Buster program is specifically designed to do the following:

1. Empower each employee in the district with an opportunity to recommend a cost saving measure directly to the superintendent.
2. Establish a direct link between the employee making the recommendation and the superintendent's office, providing a shared decision-making activity for addressing budget reductions.
3. Recognize well thought out recommendations and reward employees whose recommendations are implemented.
4. Increase face-to-face communication between employees, their supervisors, and the superintendent's office.

A major benefit of the Cost Buster program, in addition to the potential cost savings, is that all employees begin to think of their work place in a different way. Clearly, embarking on a Cost Buster program is a change in the status quo and can only be successful if the leadership, in this instance the superintendent and school board, encourage, support, and promote the activity.

Establishing a Cost Buster program requires clear guidelines. Several important ones are:

1. Appointment of a facilitator, trusted by the superintendent, to manage the implementation of the Cost Buster program. (Note: In larger districts, this individual may need a small committee to assist in implementing the process. The number of recommendations, the ability to complete a cost analysis for the recommendations, may exceed what one individual can accomplish. The flowchart found in the worksheets uses the language of "a committee;" smaller districts may wish to simply use the facilitator.)
2. A well thought out process that provides supervisors of specific areas an opportunity to support a recommendation or indicate difficulties that might occur if a given recommendation were to be implemented.
3. A provision for overriding the supervisor's analysis by the facilitator, committee, or the superintendent.
4. A clear set of guidelines, compatible with the overall budget reduction process, that encourages employees to make strong recommendations, with assurance that if recommendations achieve "real" savings and do not hamper district operations they will be supported by the superintendent.
5. A stack of Cost Buster suggestion cards should be available to all employees. (See the chapter worksheets for a suggested form.)
6. A commitment that no recommendation will be approved or denied without written documentation as to why the idea was approved or did not meet the review criteria.
7. A flowchart should be prepared that clearly outlines the process for submitting recommendations, supervisor analysis, the final decision, and recognition for approved recommendations (See chapter worksheets for an example.)

To be successful a Cost Buster program should be promoted as it is implemented. It is not enough to simply send a memo to employees about a "suggestion box." The superintendent must stress the importance of individual employee recommendations and that they will be taken seriously. In addition, the building, department, and district administrators must be committed to encouraging employees with the message of "we need your help." Further, administrators must review each recommendation with the same seriousness as the employee who submitted it. This is particularly critical as some employees may submit a recommendation to simply test the process. Finally, the school board must also support the program and encourage employees to recommend budget reductions that will achieve budget savings.

But it is not enough simply to put a program in motion. Follow-up activities are necessary to keep the program moving smoothly. A weekly "Cost Buster Hotline" publication can be used to publicize how many suggestions were received, how many were approved, the actual dollar amounts saved, and the names of the individuals who made the recommendation. A recognition ceremony is also useful. One possible way to do this is to present a Certificate of Merit to the recommending individual at a school board meeting. Another might be to secure outside funding of monetary rewards for suggestions that are approved and implemented. In two separate districts, the chamber of commerce provided recognition awards ranging from cash awards ($25 to $500 was awarded, with larger awards given for larger savings) to merchandise or service awards (examples included free meals at restaurants, gift certificates at stores, discounts for purchases, coupon packets for required services, or other specific rewards.)

Some examples of successful Cost Buster recommendations from school districts include:

1. A district maintenance employee, in a district with eighty-one schools, recommended purchase of different generator belts for motors, with no loss of quality, for half what the district was paying. While the savings were not large, new belts were provided to all schools when replacements were needed.
2. A school recommended an energy conservation program, with a portion of the savings being returned to the school. A program was initiated with 60 percent of the savings going to the district and 40 percent to the school or department. The building or department funds could be used for anything that was needed except for personnel hires. This saved a medium size district $600,000.
3. A personnel office employee recommended that principals be allowed to hire part-time persons when individuals did not want to work full time were considered. It was approved, if they were among the most qualified for the job. These suggestions gave principals greater hiring flexibility and reduced benefit costs at the same time.

Other suggestions, too numerous to detail here, were recommended by district employees. In fact, in one district 115 different recommendations were made within the first four weeks. Thirty nine percent were delayed for organizational reasons, but only twenty percent were disapproved. The impact of the Cost Buster program was felt by all employees immediately; but more importantly, the program demonstrated the seriousness of the budget cutting process. The program also provided strong evidence to the school board and the community that the district was serious about asking for advice and council during difficult times. Many of the recommendations were adopted as district practice once the crisis was over. (The energy savings recommendation is a prime example of a suggestion that became regular practice.)

So, You Have an Idea. What Now?

One final recommendation: The district needs a formal process for submitting ideas; everyone needs to follow that process using the same form. A possible form is provided in the chapter worksheets. The key idea is simple: One size fits all.

The worksheet requires that the individual or group submitting the idea take the time to use the descriptor codes detailed in chapter 11. Taking the time to make this beginning analysis, from the point of view of the individual or group, shows that the first steps in analyzing each recommendation have been utilized.

Each idea must also be submitted using the same administrative channels. Ideas must be collected at a central point in the organization. It is up to the superintendent to designate the individual within the organization who will receive all suggestions, compile them, and begin the process of completing the cost analysis described in chapter 11. The receiver of all suggestions can be the facilitator, the superintendent's secretary, or the secretary of the committee who reviews ideas. The individual is not important; the fact that everyone understands where suggestions are to be sent is vital.

Finally, the superintendent will have to establish a timeline for receiving recommendations. This presents a small problem. No one wants to exclude a good idea, but the budget reduction process demands that each step in the process be allowed adequate time for completion. So virtually every idea should be submitted by the established dates in the superintendent's timeline. The exception may be the creative suggestion that comes at a later date, but even if it is accepted late, it must go through the same evaluative process as all other ideas. Also, depending upon the nature of the crisis, the timeline may be longer or shorter. The best-case scenario, obviously, is that the district's leadership saw the crisis coming with enough lead time to do the job.

Some key points that will facilitate implementation of the Cost Buster program include:

1. The immediate supervisor provides an assessment of the suggested reduction to the employee and the committee simultaneously.
2. The Review and Analysis Committee facilitator should be responsible for collecting data from both employee and supervisor concerning the suggestion.
3. The committee may overrule the supervisor, although in most instances the data collection process facilitates decision-making in a non-confrontational manner.
4. Certificates of recognition should be awarded to all who submit recommendations regardless of committee action.
5. If possible, financial rewards should be provided for those recommendations approved. (Local businesses are often very willing to assist in this portion of the Cost Buster program.)
6. The local media should be engaged to assist with publicity to the community at large.
7. The individual(s) making successful recommendations should be recognized by the school board in some fashion.

Summary

The starting point for this chapter is also the conclusion: Ideas should be generated by the pound! This is brainstorming time and the rules for brainstorming apply. The district wants all the ideas it can get. *The fact that an idea is practical, feasible, or might save money cannot be determined if the idea has never been submitted!*

Reference

Pollard, William. Retrieved, April 13, 2009. www.DesktopQuotes.com/responsibility.

Chapter 10 Worksheets

Idea Generation

When a budget problem occurs, collect ideas from everyone to meet the goal.

Cost Buster Worksheet 1

Selling the Cost Buster program

If you are attempting to save money, it may be difficult to sell a program to the school board that will give money to employees, such as a Cost Busters Program. In addition, it makes sense to analyze any idea to see what the pros and cons of the idea might be.

Can you list five different reasons for starting your Cost Buster program?

1. _____

2. _____

3. _____

4. _____

5. _____

Or: Can you list three negatives that the board might raise? And just as importantly, after you have listed the negative, can you describe the countering point or a countering argument?

1. _____

Counter: _____

_____

2. _____

Counter: _____

_____

3. _____

Counter: _____

_____

Cost Buster Worksheet 2

Building Trust

A story is told of the Toyota car company that is illustrative of how a Cost Buster program can help your school or district. In the 1960s, when Toyota made a rather poor automobile, the employee suggestion box received only a few suggestions. But as the program grew, and the cars got better, the number of suggestions increased dramatically. In other words, as employee trust in the system developed, Toyota was able to build better cars on the strength of suggestions given by their employees.

The same idea can work for a school district that needs to restructure the budget.

Can you list five different ways to reward Cost Buster suggestions that you adopt *without* money? If times are so tough that you really don't have money for a bonus, what else can you do?

1. _____

2. _____

3. _____

4. _____

5. _____

Or: Monetary rewards are nice, and another way to reward a Cost Buster suggestion is with a bonus or a percentage of the savings. But to build trust, public acknowledgments are necessary. Therefore, list five different ways to offer public acknowledgment to a person suggesting a successful Cost Buster idea?

1. _____

2. _____

3. _____

4. _____

5. _____

Cost Buster Worksheet 3

Individual and Group Suggestions

It is important to consider two different kinds of rewards in a Cost Buster program. In one case, and individual will make a suggestion that needs to be rewarded. But in many instances a suggestion may come from an entire school or division, so the entire school or division will need to be rewarded. How can you reward the group?

In other cases, an individual might make a suggestion; but, as in the case of the building energy savings program, an entire group might have to do the work. Therefore, you might want to reward both the individual and the group, possibly at different levels.

Can you list five different ways to reward a group that makes a Cost Buster suggestion that you adopt?

1. _____

2. _____

3. _____

4. _____

5. _____

Or: How might you reward both the individual who makes the suggestion and the group that actually does the work to make the savings? Define a sample suggestion and show your rewards.

Suggestion: _____

Individual Reward:

1. _____

   _____

Group Reward:

1. _____

   _____

Cost Buster Worksheet 4

> **Common Suggestions: You can use them!**
>
> To get a Cost Buster program started, you may have to make some suggestions. It is often easiest to come up with a rather common suggestion, such as the energy savings program. Such programs have been around for almost twenty years. But one key point needs to be made: If a common suggestion saves money, isn't it a good suggestion? Therefore, to get the program rolling, you might want to suggest some routine ideas that will save money and that will be rewarded if a building uses them to save money.

Can you list five different suggestions that each building might adopt to get started saving money and that might result in rewards for the building?

1. _____

2. _____

3. _____

4. _____

5. _____

Or: Don't always rely upon your own ideas. Can you have your building or districtwide administrative or teacher team suggest some common ideas that might save money? The point here is singular: You need to get started. Now.

1. _____

2. _____

3. _____

4. _____

5. _____

Cost Buster Worksheet 5

Cost Buster Suggestion Page

Your Cost Buster suggestions will be easier to analyze if a complete suggestion is turned in. So, you might want to have a form with some common ideas that the suggestion maker needs to supply.

Can you design a Cost Buster suggestion page? Format the page with the information you feel might be important. Consider the information your district and school board would need in order to evaluate the suggestion.

_____

_____

_____

_____

_____

_____

_____

_____

_____

Cost Buster Worksheet 6

> **Cost Buster Review Committee**
>
> Your Cost Buster suggestions will have to be reviewed by the BRAC. It is important that your employees have trust in the process; that they believe a good idea may be reviewed, even after a supervisor may have turned it down. Therefore, it is vital that the committee include members that are viewed throughout the organization as being people who you can trust and people who can see the impact of a new idea.
>
> It is also important to have key members of your administrative team available to the committee. Important decisions will have to be reviewed by the administrators in charge of the areas. So, as you balance the committee, you must also name those key administrators who will advise the committee. You may want some members from the community at large, and you will need to make certain that all key advisory groups are represented.

Can you design a Cost Buster committee for your district? Try to keep the size reasonable, and try to have representatives from all necessary groups, and try to name people that have the trust of their constituents.

Member   Represents Which Group

_____   _____

_____   _____

_____   _____

_____   _____

_____   _____

_____   _____

Remember: Keep this committee small!

Cost Buster Program: From Start to Finish

An Idea Is Generated

Any employee, any citizen,
any student, anyone can generate an idea.

An Idea Is Reviewed

The idea is presented to the appropriate
department supervisor or school principal for
review and recommendation.
But an idea cannot be rejected
at this level; all suggestions need BRAC review.
Citizen suggestions go to the district office.

An Idea Is Implemented

BRAC reviews all ideas to check for adherence to base quality or essential service guidelines.
BRAC options include:

1. The idea, if recommended and agreed upon, can be implemented immediately via notification through administrative channels by the appropriate school/department.
2. If denied, the rationale is provided to the individual making the suggestion and the supervisor.
3. The committee can request that a supervisor come to the committee and present additional information, including alternative suggestions.

Then:
a. The school or department can implement immediately upon receiving approval.
b. If the idea applies to others, notification will be given to all.
c. Recognition is given to the individual making the suggestion.

An Idea (if not feasible) Is Rejected

The idea, if it does not save money, is illegal, or is not feasible, can be rejected.

a. The school or department can reject the idea immediately, and forward that decision to BRAC.
b. The districtwide committee may overturn that decision, after discussion with the supervisor.
c. The BRAC gives final rejection to the idea.
d. Documentation of the rejection must be submitted to the school board as information.

Chapter Eleven

Step 4: Internal Idea Analysis

The real voyage of discovery consists not in making new landscapes,
but in having new eyes. (Proust 2009)

Chapter Assumptions: Three assumptions underlie the ideas in this chapter.
1. Evidence based analysis of budget reduction recommendations is essential.
2. A clear set of criteria for analyzing recommended reductions reduces the likelihood of politicizing the process.
3. Analysis of recommended budget reductions should be continuous.

Chapter Objectives: The chapter has four basic objectives. The district will:
1. Establish a framework for analyzing recommendations.
2. Implement the evaluation criteria.
3. Utilize multi-level screening.
4. Prepare a decision-making package for the budget reduction committee.

Establish a Framework for Analyzing Recommendations

The quote at the beginning of this chapter must serve as the guide for this phase of the budget reduction process. Numerous individuals, and many groups, have (by this point in time) offered suggestions to address the financial crisis. The key question at this point for the superintendent is: "What impact will the recommended reductions have on the purpose of the school system?"; namely, *educating young people*.

While many of the recommended reductions will initially appear worthy of adoption, a process must be in place that requires systematic analysis of each recommendation. Sufficient evidence, including hard data, must be provided and analyzed to determine the anticipated result of a given recommendation, if implemented. Anyone (group or individual) who offers "just a thought," and who has not taken that thought through the established evaluation process has not provided sufficient information to warrant serious consideration of the idea.

Two concepts are basic: All recommendations go through the analysis phase, and all recommendations must be supported by data. If a recommendation has merit; that merit will emerge through analysis. This is true for all ideas, at all times during the process. Even if someone has a "wonderful thought" late in the total budget reduction process, that thought goes through the process. If the "thought" has merit, it can be taken back through the process for the same evaluation as every other suggestion, and the merit will be supported by real data: dollars to be saved, minimal impact upon classrooms, or maximum return in achievement.

Every reduction recommendation must be evaluated; *that is a simple rule that must be defended continuously*. The internal analysis phase of the budget reduction process is critical for these reasons:

1. To determine if all participating stakeholders have completed their work;
2. To ensure that every budget reduction suggested has been processed through the finance department to conduct a thorough analysis of actual savings;
3. To determine if a complete review of all suggested policy options has been conducted;
4. To check if the data from the community and staff survey has been accurately analyzed and is ready for reporting; and
5. To determine if potential programmatic impacts have been systematically analyzed.

Internal administrative staff are the best qualified to make the aforementioned analysis. They are the staff that has the greatest in-depth knowledge of the district and who are charged with their responsibilities by the superintendent. While this phase may be perceived as unnecessary due to expected stakeholder review when ideas are submitted for consideration; it, in fact, will not hold back the process since reviews should be continually ongoing.

The focus of this internal review should be the mission and strategic objectives of the organization. All recommendations for budget cuts should be analyzed against the mission statement and the subsequent objectives develop to meet that mission. The analysis process must require that participants "focus on the customer," namely, the youth who are served by the school district.

Accomplishment of this phase requires the superintendent to assume internal responsibility for creating a review team or teams and to oversee the way they function. The superintendent must be assured that more than one set of eyes has evaluated the data, and that the review teams utilized a systematic process for each analysis. Remember, the data and the recommendations will be reviewed again by the superintendent's budget reduction advisory committee; there should be no surprises at that time with regard to data accuracy. Individuals who directly report to the superintendent should head up each of these review teams. They should be free to select individuals from their (or other) departments to assist.

The selection of the teams to conduct the internal analysis, while determined by the superintendent and the senior leadership, should follow some general parameters. They include:

1. A member representing the implementation portion of the area (building principal, transportation area supervisor, secretary, etc.).
2. A member who has districtwide responsibility of the area for which a budget reduction has been recommended (curriculum consultant, human resource specialist, assessment specialist, etc.).
3. A member who is knowledgeable of the financial details (budget technician, accounting supervisor, internal auditor, etc.).
4. A member who keeps documentation of the team's activities.

Obviously, the larger the district, the greater the number of teams required to analyze all of the recommended reductions. Small to medium size districts may require only one team, one that analyzes every recommendation submitted. Regardless of the size of the district this evaluation/analysis step must not be avoided. A solid rationale must be established for each budget reduction item actually forwarded to the school board. The credibility of the superintendent and the budget reduction process are dependent upon complete implementation of this step in the process.

The specific individuals that become members of the analysis team or teams should be those that have demonstrated the ability to avoid the dreaded TTWWADI syndrome. (TTWWADI thinking is "That's the way we've always done it.") Instead, they must be those who are capable of new thinking, of seeing different ways to accomplish a goal. The members of the review team should be capable of examining new ideas, asking "Why not?" and of honestly considering ideas separately from the person making the suggestion, separately from the fact that it is a new way of doing something, or separately from the fact that it may require new effort on someone's part. They must be able to see change as an alternative to cutting a job, cutting a program, or in the worst case, *cutting my job*! Therefore, serious thought should go into selecting each team member and the composition of the analysis team.

Examples of analysis teams for large districts are provided here; smaller districts would combine several of these suggestions into one or more committees:

1. Team 1: Analyze direct program services; those suggestions impacting instruction to students.
2. Team 2: Analyze direct support services to instruction, focusing upon recommendations that impact curriculum personnel, testing specialists, etc.
3. Team 3: Analyze indirect instructional support, focusing upon recommendations that impact personnel services, transportation services, facilities, etc.
4. Team 4: Analyze suggestions that may impact district wide legal and financial services. This team should be led by the superintendent or at least the superintendent's chief deputy or associate.

Analysis teams should receive some overall guidance from the superintendent. This should include their mission, the timeline, a reporting process, and the analysis or evaluation criteria. All available data should be provided to each team leader and open communication lines throughout the district should be expected. A team leader is expected and encouraged to seek out new information, determine if clarification is required, and request and obtain all supporting data from any source, regardless of reporting relationships or previously established protocols.

Implementing an Evaluation Criteria

Each phase of the budget reduction process should rely upon a set of criteria developed for use by stakeholders. This results in a common language being used by participants in the process and encourages a systematic approach to solving the financial crisis. Also, with all participants using a common language, confidence is engendered in the process and a feeling of "I know what is going on" should be encouraged for everyone involved. This is critical to a budget reduction process, since confusion and distrust follow quickly when clarity of purpose and practice are not understood or not followed.

The internal analysis phase must also meet the same communication test as previous phases. Therefore, the existing common language should be utilized and any additional language or criteria that may be necessary should be framed to assist with the analysis.

The descriptor codes provided in this chapter are designed to serve as the "language" for analyzing all budget reduction recommendations. The first three code categories have been discussed in previous chapters: Base Quality Education or Essential Support; Legality; and Board Policy. These three code categories are considered "priority screen criteria" since all reduction recommendations must first be analyzed in relation to their definitions (Guiding Principle No. 2, chapter 7). The remaining three code categories are intended to focus on the impact of a reduction recommendation on district services, the instructional program, and, the feasibility of improving productivity through a change of policy, work methods, or technology. The complete list of descriptor codes is outlined below.

Example of Descriptor Codes

Base Quality Education or Essential Support Code:
1. Required by established standards
2. Referenced in established standards as being highly desirable to educational program.
3. No established standard available, although required or highly desirable. (Explain rationale.)

Legality Code:
1. Proposed reduction of services is legally permissible. No legal challenges are expected.
2. Proposed reduction in services may result in legal challenges, but probability is high that reductions can be sustained.
0. Proposed reductions in services will result in legal challenges, which we cannot defend.

Board Policy Code:
1. Proposed reduction is not governed by existing board policy.
2. Proposed reduction is permissible under existing board policy.
3. Proposed reduction is against current board policy. A challenge or exception to the policy considered appropriate and possible.
0. Proposed reduction is against current board policy. A challenge or exception is not appropriate.

Level of Service Code:
1. Elimination of service.
2. Reduction of service level.
3. Maintain essentially the same level with reduced resources.
4. Proposed transfer of responsibility and related budgeted amount.
0. Impacts a service that is required.

Impact Analysis Code:
I   Instructional services reduction.
IS   Instructional support services reduction.
IIS   Indirect instructional support services reduction.
H   High impact on district services or programs.
M   Moderate impact on district services or programs.
L   Low Impact on district services or programs.

Productivity Improvement Analysis:
1. Alternative technologies
2. Working methods
 * staffing ratios
 * procedures
3. Policy/regulations

    Each administrative team charged with internal analysis and evaluation should review the descriptor codes that have been framed. Any modification should be thoroughly discussed and only in an unusual situation should a code be refined. Once identified, no new codes should be added. If clarification is required it should be achieved with the refinement of an existing code. Only the identification of a *serious* problem should cause modification of descriptor codes once, as those descriptor codes have served and will serve as the basis for the multi-level screening process to be implemented by each analysis team. To change a code may result in asking teams to redo their work. Identifying the descriptor codes is definitely a place where *think first and act second* is necessary!

Multi-level screening

The concept of the multi-level screening process is designed to further evaluate how all recommended reductions have met the priority screen criteria. Meeting the priority screen means a reduction recommendation has satisfied the test of meeting all Base Quality or Essential Support Service requirements, all legal requirements, and all board policy requirements.

In order for the recommended reduction to be on the final list submitted to the budget advisory committee (see chapter 12), each recommended reduction must be analyzed in relation to the:

a. Level of Service Test
b. Impact Test
c. Productivity Test

This analysis will provide additional information to the advisory committee as they deliberate and make final recommendations to the school board.

Each administrative team should analyze their set of budget reduction recommendations against the descriptor codes. While appearing to be laborious, this final analysis step literally ensures that every feasible and practical consideration has been given to each recommended reduction. Further, this level of detail instills confidence in the process and provides the advisory committee information typically not available in other reduction procedures. The flowchart below represents how the process works.

Chapter 11

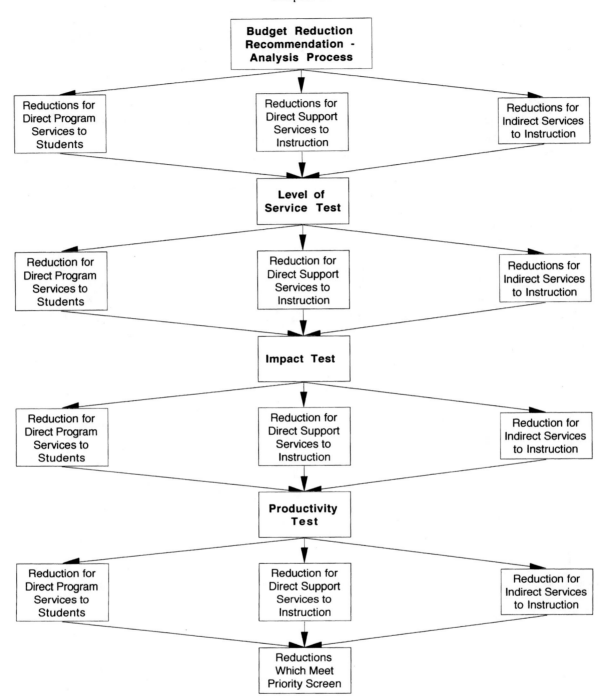

Example of the Use of Descriptor Codes

The examples provided in this chapter are intended to represent how the descriptor code system would be utilized for specific reduction recommendations. In order for the coding system to be effective some orientation of the codes is necessary. Finally, an advisory committee member may disagree with a specific code given to a specific reduction recommendation. This is to be expected. This provides an opportunity to discuss the rationale for assigning the code and further enhancing the understanding of the proposed recommended reduction. In some instances the coding can be modified to more closely reflect what advisory committee members believe would be the impact of the budget reduction, although this should be only in very rare situations.

EXAMPLE OF LEVEL 1 BUDGET REDUCTION RECOMMENDATIONS

	Description of Recommended Reduction	BP	BQE	ESS	LS	LC	IA	PIA	Reduction AMT
1	Eliminate technology upgrades	1	3	2	3	1	M	2	$228,126
2	Delay purchase of additional student assessments	1	3	3	3	1	L	NA	$107,220
3	Delay expansion of the district wellness program	1	3	3	1	1	L	3	$10,000
4	Delay in-service for Gifted & Talented teachers	1	2	NA	4	1	IS	2	$4,000

BP   Board Policy
BQE   Base Quality Education
ESS   Essential Support Service
LS   Level of Service
LC   Legality Code
IA   Impact Analysis
PIA   Productivity Impact Analysis

The representation of an application of the descriptor coding system above should clearly demonstrate its effectiveness in communicating to advisory committee members, and to the school board the specifics of recommended budget cuts. This coding system has been well received by school board members and stakeholders who have participated in the budget reduction process for the following reasons:
1. The coding system is easily understood;
2. The use of the coding system avoids unnecessary verbiage; and
3. The coding system enables all stakeholders to communicate using a common terminology.
The worksheets provide a basis for implementing the descriptor coding system.

Reference

Proust, Marcel. Retrieved February 15, 2009. www.DailyInspiringQuotes.com/attitude.

Chapter 11 Worksheets

Internal Idea Analysis

No Idea Is Accepted Until All Effects Have Been Examined.

Number	Item	Board Policy	Base Quality Education	Essential Support Services	Level of Service	Legality Code	Impact Analysis	Productivity Improvement Analysis	Reduction Amount
	Abbreviation	**BP**	**BQE**	**ESS**	**LS**	**LC**	**IP**	**PT**	

Budget Reduction: Most Immediate Budget Cuts

		Budget Reduction: Most Probable Budget Cuts							
Number	Item	Board Policy	Base Quality Education	Essential Support Services	Level of Service	Legality Code	Impact Analysis	Productivity Improvement Analysis	Reduction Amount
	Abbreviation	**BP**	**BQE**	**ESS**	**LS**	**LC**	**IP**	**PT**	

Number	Item	Board Policy	Base Quality Education	Essential Support Services	Level of Service	Legality Code	Impact Analysis	Productivity Improvement Analysis	Reduction Amount
	Abbreviation	**BP**	**BQE**	**ESS**	**LS**	**LC**	**IP**	**PT**	

Budget Reduction: Worst-Case Scenario Budget Cuts

Chapter Twelve

Step 5: Staff/Community Evaluation

Solo decision making is giving way to collective decision-making.
The manager's role is shifting from making decisions to empowering others
to make decisions. Those most knowledgeable and closest to the problem
are becoming key to the decision making process. (Saint and Lawson 1994)

Chapter Assumptions: Two assumptions form the basis of this chapter.
1. Two or more heads, given accurate information, are better than one.
2. Stakeholder commitment to the process is essential to participation.

Chapter Objectives: The objectives for this chapter include four basic ideas.
1. Establish a Budget Reduction Advisory Committee (BRAC).
2. Create ground rules for advisory committee decision-making.
3. Determine recommended reductions.
4. Submit a reduction package to the school board.

Establish a Budget Reduction Advisory Committee

The quote at the beginning of this chapter characterizes the decision-making process for achieving budget reductions. Throughout this manual a philosophy of involvement and collaboration has been the thread of each step in the reduction process. This process has been designed to empower stakeholders in a community with a key interest in school district operations. Opportunities are to be afforded to all, active involvement is suggested for recommending reductions, evaluating reductions for immediate implementation, and implementation of plans for long-term cost savings.

Suggestions are best taken in bulk. They can be immediate and suggested by anyone, such as different Cost Buster proposals, or they may focus on long-term budget reductions and may require the involvement and commitment of everyone, such as a districtwide plan for energy conservation. Or they may involve responding to a parent who asked, "Since all those wind farms are being built in our valley, do you suppose we could get one?" The resulting schoolwide project, designed to seek a grant and incorporate the entire project into the curriculum, helped one K-8 school obtain funds to (a) build a wind powered electrical generating tower, (b) use the energy generated in the school, and (c) sell power to the utility company when it was not needed by the school. Operating the tower, servicing it, monitoring the utility school's electrical bill, and comparing bills from before and after building the tower, all of these tasks became part of the curriculum/activity program for the school.

Support for a process of idea generation, evaluation, and implementation is necessary from all the board, superintendent, district senior leadership, teachers, bargaining units, employee associations, and, community stakeholders. The message through all steps of the process suggested in this manual has been and must be: *The leader, think superintendent, believes in and is committed to collaborative decision making.* The suggestion here is to act in such a way that the superintendent has been the exemplar of this leadership principle.

As noted by the authors of *Empowerment Takes More Than a Minute* (Peters, Carl, and Randolph, 1996, p. 15), "the first key is to share information with everyone." Step 3 of the reduction process provided opportunities to all stakeholders for generating cost savings and realizing additional revenue. Step 4 included a process for analyzing the cost-benefit of each recommended reduction, including having the finance department actually compute savings that would be achieved from each recommendation, and then submitting the idea to district staff who provided clarification, additional information and historical references. Such information is then given to either the individual or group making or submitting the recommendation or to the decision-making groups evaluating the recommendation.

Permeating the implementation of the process has been the philosophy that "we" have a problem, not that "you" have a problem. Team building within the process has been a value to be promoted from the first meeting with the school board through the establishment of a Cost Buster program to the evaluation of recommendations by teams of staff.

The next element of this collaborative process is to develop a way in which representatives from all stakeholders can receive a complete package of the targeted budget reductions, review the data for each recommendation, and provide the superintendent with final advice and counsel prior to submission of the reduction package to the school board. The creation of a Budget Reduction Advisory Committee (BRAC) is the vehicle provided for Step 5 in the process.

Membership of the BRAC should include representatives from each stakeholder group that has been involved with generating budget reduction recommendations. The membership would include, but may not be limited, to the following groups:

1. Teacher bargaining group
2. Support staff bargaining groups (teamsters, electrical workers, etc.)
3. Employee associations (clerical, nutrition, etc.)
4. Building principals
5. Each district program advisory committee (gifted/talented, vocational, etc.)
6. Board advisory committees (long-range planning, etc.)
7. District, county, or other designation for the local PTO groups and Citizens Committees.
8. Military representative, if a military base or post is in the locale.
9. An at-large representative from each school board election zone, appointed by each board member (optional).

> Author's Note: District level personnel should not be members of the BRAC. But they should always be available to provide clarification on any proposed budget reduction.

Each stakeholder group should select their representative to the BRAC. To do otherwise will detract from the collaborative leadership principle and engender mistrust. Some representatives may be more outspoken than what may be desired, or some may have been critics of the school board, superintendent, or the district in general. The belief here is simple: It is better to have them at the table raising their questions or voicing their concerns than to have them outside of the committee process without accurate information, waiting to raise issues during the final stages of the process. The local situation will dictate the number and type of representatives for service on the BRAC; committee membership may change from district to district. Each stakeholder group's number of representatives will also depend on the size of the district and the local political environment.

Inviting organizations to select representatives should include some explanation of the purpose of the BRAC. The primary purpose is to achieve consensus on the budget reductions that will be presented to the school board. Saint and Lawson (1994) in their book, entitled *Rules for Reaching Consensus: A Modern Approach to Decision Making*, describe it as "A state of mutual agreement among members of a group where all legitimate concerns of individuals have been addressed to the satisfaction of the group." p. 21.

Therefore, the specific purposes of the BRAC, while they may change slightly from district to district, should generally include:

1. To review the draft budget reduction package for each of the reduction levels, the most immediate, the most probable, and the worst-case scenarios.
2. To provide information and respond to questions from BRAC members on any and all proposed reductions.
3. To achieve consensus on as many of the reduction recommendations as possible.
4. To secure additional information, with the time available, on any recommended reduction that may cause substantial concern from any stakeholder group.
5. To consider any additional reduction recommendations that may have arisen since the reduction package was prepared.
6. To finalize a package of reduction recommendations for submission to the school board.

As BRAC members will work together to address the problem at hand, general patterns of behavior should be employed. Saint and Lawson (1994) provide much needed guidance. They suggest that good interpersonal relationships between group members should be encouraged; that each member listen to and try to understand another members point of view; and that members should remember the purpose of the deliberation is to achieve consensus. It is the responsibility of all participants to foster and demonstrate the aforementioned attitudes and behaviors. However, no group or individual has a greater responsibility to ensure adherence to these guidelines than the superintendent and district staff.

Key to the whole process has been the avoidance of solo decision-making by any person or group. Consensus decision-making has been the goal. The superintendent's role is to facilitate the process. Stakeholders should know the expectations and be allowed to operate within the expectations in a free and open manner. Some questions that should be asked of all participants as the process moves to completion are:

1. What is our primary purpose as an organization?
2. What are our operational guidelines for decision-making?
3. How can key goals and results be achieved given the current circumstances?
4. What does the future hold if the current recommendations are implemented?

Ground Rules for Decision-Making

Once the BRAC has been formed, the superintendent should call the first meeting to cover the following points:

1. Establish the rules for decision-making;
2. Review the complete budget reduction package; and
3. Establish a time-line for decision-making.

The superintendent as facilitator should conduct this meeting and review the complete six-step process, the current status of the process, the descriptor codes, rating summaries, and the cost savings and/or revenue enhancement goals. This stage setting is especially important, as the information will initially tend to overwhelm committee members if time is not set aside to review all stages of the process and the role they will play in making a final set of recommendations to the school board. Committee should be informed of the options if consensus cannot be reached on a set of final budget reduction recommendations. This would include, but not be limited to, the superintendent adjourning the committee and submitting a list of recommendations to the school board without committee support. In this instance, committee members would be free to speak to the school board on those recommendations they support or do not support. Always the goal is to achieve consensus.

Committee members should then be provided time, outside of the meeting, to review and analyze all recommended reductions and revenue enhancements. As committee members are representatives of a variety of stakeholder groups, both within and outside the district, they will want to confer with other members of the group they represent. This is particularly critical as each group of representatives should be prepared to speak for the group they represent. As a result, they will need some time to discuss the reduction package with their group. The process is designed to avoid a rush to judgment. Even in a crisis situation some time should be provided for thoughtful examination of available options.

The second meeting of the advisory committee is designed to address points of clarification, concern and/or reordering the rank ordered reductions. The setting for this meeting is even more critical than the first meeting. All committee members should be able to see each other, writing materials should be provided, a finance department member should be available to compute actual cost savings, and an easel should be available with a staff member assigned to record each committee decision. Even if computer projection equipment is used to show the various recommendations, a paper (or chalkboard) record acts as a constantly visible "scorecard" as the committee moves through its agenda.

The meeting should begin with a reminder of the ground rules. Next, questions, concerns, and points of clarification should be addressed. These should only be the concerns that are new since the first meeting. If any single concern becomes a major impediment to moving the group forward, the superintendent should request that discussion on that concern raised be delayed, or request the group to vote to determine if additional time should be spent on the issue. However, votes on any budget reduction recommendation, at this stage of the process, should be avoided at all costs. Remember: consensus is the goal. Time should be spent on each recommendation, each issue, and each conclusion. Once an item is identified for a special vote the mentality of the group changes from "we are in this together" to each group pushing their own agenda, especially if the group has not put in the time to make the decision their own.

Once the question/concern phase of the second meeting is completed the superintendent should request official consensus on the process, general goals, and such specifics as meeting time and place. Once this has been established, it is time to turn to the actual budget reduction recommendations.

Determining Recommended Reductions

Each recommendation should be considered fully; if consensus can be reached, then the group moves on to the next. If consensus is not achieved, then each item of recommended reductions should be addressed singularly. Typically, the advisory committee will agree to major expenditure reductions and offer a refinement of an existing recommendation.

An example of this occurred in a situation where special education teacher aides were to be reduced in numbers and much discussion ensued as to their value. Seeing that the committee required more justification from a member who wanted to retain them, another member, representing a teacher bargaining group, indicated an increase in the pupil-teacher ratio (PTR) should be another, separate item. Seeing movement, some principals asked if the individual was recommending an increase in PTR for general education or special education teachers. Noting it was for general education teachers only, the group agreed to the revision and moved to other issues. This example demonstrates that all members need not agree to every point in a proposal, but may suggest modifications, and that consensus may come from a combination of ideas.

The committee should move through the total proposal, either in general segments or in item by item discussions, and come to consensus on the recommendations. It may be necessary to reinforce the committee's purpose or assess individual matters collectively, but this is usually accomplished as the group moves forward. The superintendent should be attuned to this potential occurrence and should be able to handle it in a rather routine manner without disturbing the group discussion. The charts provided below illustrate the process base the BRAC should use for their decision-making.

The first chart covers what is called the "Most Immediate Needs" for budget cuts. If an emergency situation occurred, where cuts were demanded during the existing year's budget, these would be the first cuts made in District B.

	Budget Reduction: Most Immediate Budget Cuts								
Number	**Item**	Board Policy	Base Quality Education	Essential Support Services	Level of Service	Legality Code	Impact Analysis	Productivity Improvement Analysis	Reduction Amount
	Abbreviation	**BP**	**BQE**	**ESS**	**LS**	**LC**	**IA**	**PIA**	
1	Eliminate Technology Upgrade	1	3	1	2	1	IS/M	2	$228,126
2	Delay Purchase of Additional Student Assessments	1	3	3	3	1	IS/L	NA	$107,220
3	Delay Expansion of District Wellness Program	1	3	3	1	1	IIS-L	3	$10,000
4	Delay In-service for Gifted and Talented Teachers	1	2	2	4	1	IS/M	2	$4,000
Total Budget Reductions									**$349,346**

The numbers and/or letters in the individual boxes all come from the descriptor codes found in chapter 11. The codes for item 1, Eliminate Technology Upgrade, can be explained as: A "1" in board policy shows the school board of District B has no approved policy on technology upgrades. (This may differ by school district. For example, a different board established regulations on the cost of an upgrade as opposed to the repair or service of existing equipment.) The "3" in the Base Quality Education column shows that "there are established standards available, but the upgrade is highly desirable. As can be seen from these examples, the number/letter content of each box comes directly from the descriptor codes.

But each item should be thoroughly considered and or discussed to reach consensus on the rating; no one individual should assign code values.

Chart 2 shows how the cuts would grow in the "most probable situation."

	Item	Board Policy	Base Quality Education	Essential Support Services	Level of Service	Legality Code	Impact Analysis	Productivity Improvement Analysis	Reduction Amount
Number	**Abbreviation**	**BP**	**BQE**	**ESS**	**LS**	**LC**	**IA**	**PIA**	
1	Eliminate Technology Upgrade	1	3	1	2	1	IS/M	2	$228,126
2	Delay Purchase of Additional Student Assessments	1	3	3	3	1	IS/L	NA	$107,220
3	Delay Expansion of District Wellness Program	1	3	3	1	1	IIS-L	3	$10,000
4	Delay In-service for Gifted and Talented Teachers	1	2	2	4	1	IS/M	2	$4,000
5	Freeze Teacher Salaries	3	3	3	3	2	3/L	2	$217,000
6	Fringe Benefit Savings	3	3	3	3	2	3/L	2	$58,590
7	High School Hire Freeze	2	3	3	1	1	I/L	2	$58,000
8	Hire Freeze Benefits	2	3	3	1	1	I/L	2	$21,660
Total Budget Reductions									**$704,596**

Budget Reduction: Most Probable Budget Cuts

First, note the code information for Items 1 through 4 remains the same. The four new items each have code values attached. To explain the reasoning, consider Item 5, the freezing of teacher salaries. The 3/L in the impact column can be used to explain District B's situation. The "3" indicates the same service will be maintained; the "L" means that the impact should be low. The reasoning for the "L" is important. If the budget crisis has been thoroughly communicated and understood by all involved, teachers should see the logic of "no pay raise" is preferable over the loss of existing teaching positions, combined with the then necessary increase in class size. Others might argue that the ranking should be "M," indicating a moderate impact. District B teachers did not.

The high school hiring freeze has a low impact for a singular reason. It deals with the cutting of one position, where the teacher retired. Reducing the number of elective choices available to students makes the cut possible at a low impact level. All of the electives that were cut were small enrollment classes.

One special note: the fringe benefit ratings for Items 6 and 8 are the same as the salary lines 5 and 7. In other words, the fringe benefits are tied to the salary lines. The codes for Item 6 and 8, therefore, are not debatable; they are the same as Items 5 and 7, which are debatable. This is the type of discussion that should accompany each item, and it is necessary that every member of the BRAC understands the assigned codes. If the BRAC has questions, the individual and/or team member responsible for the coding should explain, if not defend, their choice of code ratings.

The final chart provides suggestions for the worst-case scenario.

Budget Reduction: Worst-Case Scenario Budget Cuts									
Number	Item	Board Policy	Base Quality Education	Essential Support Services	Level of Service	Legality Code	Impact Analysis	Productivity Improvement Analysis	Reduction Amount
	Abbreviation	BP	BQE	ESS	LS	LC	IA	PIA	
1	Eliminate Tech Upgrade	1	3	1	2	1	IS/M	2	$228,126
2	Delay Purchase of Student Assessments	1	3	3	3	1	IS/L	NA	$107,220
3	Delay Wellness Program	1	3	3	1	1	IIS-L	3	$10,000
4	Delay G/T In-service	1	2	NA	4	1	IS/M	2	$4,000
5	Freeze Teacher Salaries	3	3	3	3	2	3/L	2	$217,000
6	Fringe Benefit Savings	3	3	3	3	2	3/L	2	$58,590
7	High School Hire Freeze	2	3	3	1	1	1/L	2	$58,000
8	Hire Freeze Benefits	2	3	3	1	1	1/L	2	$21,660
9	Cut Field Trip Travel	1	3	3	1	1	IS/M	1	$150,679
10	Cut Distance Learning	1	3	3	1	2	I/H	1	$25,000
11	Cut Substitute Teachers	2	3	3	1	1	IS/M	2	$212,000
Total Budget Reductions									$1,092,275

Note that all the cuts from the most immediate and most probable charts are still included, but three additional cuts have been suggested. The ranking of these suggestions could be debated. Why was salary freeze recommended before cutting field trips. The logic belongs to District B, but it included the following: Field trips impact the classroom and learning; distance learning provides advanced classes and is part of an existing contract with the nearby university. But the impact of both of these cuts is approximately $100,000 less than the freezing of salaries. The salary freeze provides a large reduction in costs with a relatively low impact, as seen by District B. Others might argue.

The district's application of the rating codes is clearly dependent upon a variety of factors, including board policies, state laws, community values, the attitudes of different bargaining units, and the philosophy of the district leaders. The coding system is designed to deal with facts and to have these educational/political discussions at the lowest level possible where the primary focus is to have minimal impact upon the classroom. If these decisions came to the board, without coding, then all of the political discussion would take place in the public session of a school board meeting. This means several things. There would be little or no factual input; most individuals would be arguing feelings. Second, having minimal impact upon the classroom would not be the defining position of most making statements to the board.

Using the codes given at the lowest possible level gives board members a very logical response to pose to anyone arguing against the recommendations. *If you disagree with the reduction and the code ratings, give the board another recommendation for a cut or set of cuts that is equal in size and would result in similar code ratings.*

In districts that have used this complete budget reduction process, the response by board members given above has clarified the debates with factual information as opposed to feelings. Most always, a late recommendation to change the final budget cuts had already been suggested, considered, rejected or placed further down any list of suggested cuts, due to the committee discussions preceding the submission of the final suggestions to the school board.

Experience has shown that if sufficient preparation has occurred, the superintendent can keep the group on task and individual or group concerns can be addressed and consensus can be achieved. In one school district, for example, a reduction of approximately $17 million was achieved without a single recommendation for change. The budget advisory committee approved for recommendation to the board all of the budget suggestions that came through the budget reduction process. In addition, eight bargaining groups (with membership on this committee) also approved the recommendations without change. Consensus was achieved because of extensive preplanning, stakeholder involvement, and shared decision-making. These were the recommendations of everyone; one single individual or group did not own the recommendations. Essentially, consensus was reached as the recommendations were made; the BRAC simply provided oversight while completing the entire list.

It is possible that the budget advisory committee will not reach consensus. The superintendent must consider this possibility and plan for it. What options exist? The options available to the committee and superintendent are somewhat limited when budget evaluations are in order. The four most usable have proven to be (1) limited additional time, (2) rearrangement of evaluation rankings, (3) the introduction of a new reduction recommendation, (4) and/or the superintendent withdrawing those segments of the proposal that cannot be agreed upon and indicating the removed recommendations will be submitted as his recommendation without committee consensus. Limited additional time may be offered if new information becomes available or the required time frame for decision-making had some flexibility built in at the outset. Experience has demonstrated this is difficult to achieve.

More probable is a rearrangement of priorities for budget reduction until a given consensus level is achieved. Consensus may fail because of the order in which the reductions are ranked. For example, a recommendation that a specific budget reduction/cut be ranked higher (or lower) might solve the consensus problem. In one district, when it became necessary to increase the pupil/teacher ratio, the teacher's bargaining unit supported the increase if special education aides were retained.

From time to time consensus may be reached only after the introduction of a new option, one previously not available. An example would be the decision by a legislature to enact an early retirement incentive program not available for consideration earlier. This occurred in one district; pending legislation was approved after the district was well into the consensus decision-making process. The new legislation presented a new opportunity which the district seized. The budget advisory committee suspended its deliberations until the cost/benefit information on early retirements became available for committee review. The final analysis made it possible for the district to reduce the list of recommended budget reductions. (In another school district, however, the same option of early retirement was provided by the legislature, but the cost/benefit analysis revealed that it would not help the district. The district mostly employed younger employees who were not eligible.)

It is entirely possible the committee might not reach agreement on the total package of reduction recommendations. In this event an option is for the superintendent to recess the committee, determine a final list of reduction options, return to the committee to inform the committee of the final list. This possibility does not require the consensus process, as the superintendent is taking charge only after consensus has failed.

Submitting a Reduction Package to the School Board

The ultimate goal of the BRAC is to prepare and submit a final list of budget reduction recommendations to the board. This may occur in one of several ways. Obviously, the hoped for procedure is that the committee will reach consensus on its list of recommendations and submit their list directly to the board. But if all of the options noted fail in helping the BRAC reach consensus, recommendations still must go forward to the school board. This will necessitate dismissal of the committee and the final reduction recommendations submitted to the board in two segments: 1) Those recommendations reached by consensus; and 2) those recommendations not agreed upon by consensus but submitted separately by the superintendent to balance the budget.

The final position of the superintendent must be that "the buck stops here." If consensus cannot be reached in the BRAC, the superintendent is still responsible for presenting a balanced budget. However, in those districts where the entire process has been completely utilized, this action has never been required. But notice the emphasis upon the "complete" application of the "entire" process. It takes time, effort, and a willingness to work together by everyone involved. But when the severity of the budget emergency is understood and accepted by all, the process has worked. But picking just a portion of the process, in order to find shortcuts to a solution, will not get the job done.

One final comment on the effectiveness of the Step 5 process must be added. One school district, with 8 bargaining units and 7,000 employees, achieved consensus on budget reductions totaling $42.2M million over a 12 month period. Further, all 8 bargaining groups testified to the school board about the effectiveness of the process and strongly urged the school board to avoid tampering with any of the recommended reductions, including their rank order. The school board, with one small exception, voted to unanimously accept the recommendations of the superintendent and the BRAC. Needless to say, this process avoided a potential for development of major divisions among employee groups and the community at large. An experienced building principal explained the success of the process with this statement: "If the process had not worked, the superintendent would have been considered a failure. Since it worked, the superintendent was considered a hero."

References:

Blanchard, Kenneth, John P. Carolos, and Alan Randolph (1996). San Francisco, CA: *Empowerment Takes under a Minute.* Barrett-Kockler Publishers.

Saint, Steven and James R. Lawson (1994). *Rules for Reaching Consensus: A Modern Approach to Decision-Making.* San Diego, CA: Pfeiffer and Company.

Chapter 12 Worksheets

Staff/Community Evaluation

Everything is evaluated by all stakeholder groups.

General Work Rules for the BRAC

1. All communications consider issues, not individuals. Avoid naming names in all situations.

2. Accept any suggestions at face value; don't look for hidden agendas.

3. Accept all suggestions when offered; you then may reject any that do not meet the defined criteria.

4. Respect all comments by actively listening to the ideas presented.

5. Equality of membership is vital; equality of ideas is also vital. Everyone and everything receives the same examination.

6. Reject stereotyped positions: (Examine with data, not opinions. Everyone communicates; no one hides.) Stereotyped positions may include:

    a. "We'll hide in our hole and wait this one out."
    b. "Our school can't survive without this program."
    c. "I have the information; I'll get back to you."
    d. "I have the money and I'll take care of you."
    e. "We'll just send a memo; I don't want to face them."
    f. "The ___ made me do that." (Fill in the name of the appropriate group or organization.)

7. Work with clear language, not technical or professional jargon.

8. Represent your true patrons (teachers and children), not special interest groups.

9. Use the tough love concept; disagree when needed without being disagreeable.

10. In the final analysis, everyone must accept that there are "no excuses, just solutions" when attempting to communicate.

Number	Item	Board Policy	Base Quality Education	Essential Support Services	Level of Service	Legality Code	Impact Analysis	Productivity Improvement Analysis	Reduction Amount
	Budget Reduction: Most Immediate Budget Cuts								
	Abbreviation	BP	BQE	ESS	LS	LC	IP	PT	
Total Budget Reductions									

Number	Item	Board Policy	Base Quality Education	Essential Support Services	Level of Service	Legality Code	Impact Analysis	Productivity Improvement Analysis	Reduction Amount
	Budget Reduction: Most Probable Budget Cuts								
	Abbreviation	**BP**	**BQE**	**ESS**	**LS**	**LC**	**IP**	**PT**	
Total Budget Reductions									

Budget Reduction: Worst-Case Scenario Budget Cuts

Number	Item	Board Policy	Base Quality Education	Essential Support Services	Level of Service	Legality Code	Impact Analysis	Productivity Improvement Analysis	Reduction Amount
	Abbreviation	BP	BQE	ESS	LS	LC	IP	PT	
Total Budget Reductions									

Chapter Thirteen

Step 6: School Board Involvement

People without information cannot act responsibly.
People with information are compelled to act responsibly.
(Blanchard, Carols, and Randolph 1996)

Chapter Assumptions: Three basic assumptions underlie the suggestions in this chapter.
1. The school board and superintendent must serve as the exemplars of the process.
2. Decision-making ground rules by the school board are critical to the success of the process.
3. The final reduction package must reflect the implementation of the process.

Chapter Objectives: The role of the school board is to:
1. Acquire the required background knowledge for making reduction decisions.
2. Approve ground rules for decision-making.
3. Obtain additional citizen input, if community members wish to give input.
4. Take action.
5. Deal with the aftermath, including working to obtain community support for the final budget.

Acquiring Knowledge for Reduction Decisions

The preliminary work for budget reduction, although extensive, should now be complete. School district staff, internal and external stakeholders, and budget advisory committee members have studied all reduction recommendations and prioritized the final list for submission to the school board. This may not be familiar to most boards and superintendents, since it generally does not mirror what is done to build a budget or reduce a budget. Most superintendents are familiar with incrementally increasing budgets based on the cost of living or the infusion of new dollars.

Fortunate is the district that receives major new income sources, through oil or timber revenues, major business or factory startups, infusion of state or federal impact funds, or something that causes a substantial increase in property assessments. Most administrators are familiar with these forms of budget increases. But few are experienced with substantial restructuring or reducing budgets during difficult financial times.

The authors have found that a majority of the developmental work in preparing budgets is accomplished by internal staff, with little or no input from bargaining groups, employee association, citizens or advisory groups. If this is the case in your district, serious work needs to be done before a process like the one described in this manual will be successful. In some districts structures and processes have become so entrenched that most feel they cannot be changed. People who are knowledgeable about educational change would strongly agree with this point. Therefore, at this stage of the process, every effort should be made to use the original, complete foundation of the system for budget reduction.

Packaging the decision options for the school board is essential if the board is to acquire sufficient understanding of the budget reductions recommended to make decisions. Materials provided the board at this juncture should include:

1. A comparison of the continuation budget with the contingency budget to find the amount of the required reduction;
2. An overview of the process resulting in the recommended reductions;
3. The net impact on local and state revenue figures;
4. The key elements of the recommended reductions; and
5. The net impact on the mission of the school district.

The background information to be provided to the board is most important, and it is not usually part of the budget package. But the board needs to understand the work that has gone into completing the recommended budget, the agreements that have been reached in order to obtain consensus, and the support that exists for the final recommendation. In addition, the board should be aware of the impact of cuts (or categories of cuts) will have on school services. Examples would range from (1) increasing the pupil teacher ratio across the entire district or (2) a specific reduction in one identified program or service. The point is that board members should understand the impacts, as school patrons *will* call when one of the cuts impacts their children.

The summary sheets that were prepared and included in the total package of materials presented to the board (see chapter 12) identified specific reductions and utilized the descriptor codes to provide background information to each group participating in the process. All of this material, if possible, should be distributed to the school board, employee groups, the media, budget advisory committee members, and other interested individuals at least one week in advance of the first public session to address the reductions.

At this point a focus on information management is important for the board, superintendent and the general public. Education is an information intensive activity; the amount of information available to all stakeholders can become overwhelming and therefore meaningless. Clear, concise information is the goal. Even though the budget reduction process is critical and all information necessary for effective board decision-making should be provided, *executive summaries covering each decision package should be provided*. It is obviously helpful if the board has already agreed to the process, the information to be given to them, and the format for decision-making. The superintendent should personally review each decision package prior to providing it to the board.

The first public meeting for the school board should be a work session. This session is not designed for action, but for the board to obtain a thorough understanding of the recommended reductions and the rationale for each recommendation. Critical to this phase is the presentation to the school board of the descriptions for base quality education and essential support services. If these descriptions are clearly understood future board sessions should go smoothly.

The superintendent should personally address the overall executive summary and the key recommendations. Although appearing to be obvious to some, the authors' experience is that too many times superintendents leave this important phase to the finance officer. This activity is not about finances, even though a budget reduction is eminent. This process is about how the district will educate the youth they are to serve, and how decisions will be made that impact how children are educated. Effective superintendents will emphasize the positive results of the reduction process first. One superintendent highlighted the fact that the process resulted in actually reducing the pupil teacher ratio in one area with a realignment of dollars from savings in other areas. Another superintendent emphasized that the reduction enabled the district to move more aggressively to site-based management through restructuring of districtwide services. Regardless of the specific items to be emphasized, the superintendent, as Chief

Education Officer of the district, should focus first and foremost on the issues that directly relate to students. In addition, it is always important to stress positives, even in difficult financial times.

Once the superintendent has provided the executive summary, and depending on the size of the district and the programs operated, the team leader of each reduction package work group should outline recommended reductions for their area of responsibility. A time limit should be established for each one of these presentations in order for them not to become unfocused. In fact, each presentation should be practiced in front of the superintendent and key staff members prior to the board work session. A guiding principle for the superintendent at this point might be summarized as follows. While the superintendent presents to the board, he or she empowers key staff members to make specific, effective presentations on the details of the budget reduction recommendations of their work groups, as approved by the total Budget Reduction Advisory Committee.

Depending upon available technical and human resources, the board's first work session should be televised so that interested citizens can view the superintendent's presentation, hear the school board's questions, and listen to the administrators' responses to those questions. This also assists the board members in meeting their obligations for open government. The work session affords the opportunity for the administration to determine if there are major questions raised by the board that need to be further researched prior to any actual vote being taken.

Once the work session has covered all aspects of information and clarification, a portion of the session should be focused on the ground rules for public testimony and board deliberation at the next public meeting. While no action should be taken at the work session, the staff and community deserve to understand the board's thinking on the issues.

Creating Ground Rules for Decision-Making

Conducting a budget reduction decision meeting is like no other board meeting. Jobs, programs, and careers may be at stake. Emotions can run high. If the planning process has been thoroughly implemented, these emotional reactions should be minimized. However, unrest can appear at any time because of the highly volatile nature of the issues being discussed. Advanced planning is therefore critical. Depending upon the local situation, the superintendent, working in conjunction with the board, may need security present at the meeting. It is critical that the school board reach agreement on decision-making guidelines in advance of an open session. In addition, guidelines regarding public testimony and recommendations made by the general public must be in place. In other words, since the issues will be volatile, the process for dealing with them should be quietly and firmly established. The process should be solid, especially when decisions and discussions are difficult.

Some decision guidelines are fairly easy to establish. Returning to the "guiding principles" outlined in chapter 7 should be the starting point for the board. Three of the guiding principles should be the focus of board discussions and testimony to the board:

No 5: Budget Reduction Proposals Must Be Targeted to Real, Achievable Ends.

No 6: A Budget Cut Recommended to the Board by the Review Process Can be Omitted Only If Another Budget Cut of a Similar Dollar Amount Is Substituted.

No 7: Percentage or Across the Board Cuts Should Be Avoided.

Experience, however, has shown there are other decision rules that can have a significant impact on board deliberations. The school board must consider and implement decision-making guidelines that sustain the integrity of the budget reduction process. The following items have been tested in school board meetings and have worked for those school boards:

1. Board members recommending reductions must meet the same criteria as all other reduction recommendations, i.e., they must use the same guiding principles and they must use the same descriptor codes, etc., so that others may understand the impact of their new recommendations;
2. Board member recommendations must be evaluated by the finance department to determine actual

savings. Therefore, they cannot be made and acted upon at the same meeting. (This is only fair; all other recommendations had to withstand a cost analysis.);

3. Community or staff members recommendations or modifications, made at the school board meeting, must meet the same criteria as all other recommended actions or the recommendation will *not* be considered at the same meeting in which they are suggested. (In other words, no individual or group may present an undocumented proposal at the board meeting and expect consideration of that proposal until it has gone through the same process as every other suggestion.); and,

4. If criteria 1-3 are insufficient to cover a question, the board will return to the major assumptions and guiding principles as the basis for their decision.

A key point must be made here: *At this late date, new suggestions must be considered as dangerous.* Late suggestions, and therefore changes to the budget, may upset the delicate balance that brought consensus on the final list of recommendations; they may undermine and therefore remove support from the budget reduction package submitted to the board. If new suggestions are to be considered, *they must go back through the entire process.*

While appearing to be difficult to achieve, these decision guidelines are as important to school board members as they are to those actively involved in submitting new reduction recommendations. No public official wants to look bad to constituents; and, if these board members are included in the reasoning process behind the guidelines, they will usually agree on this issue. However, there is always an individual or group who will attempt to pressure a board member to go outside the process and take another direction. Obviously, the board as a body can only discipline itself or it's members. The role of the superintendent, if this occurs, is to constantly remind the board of the process it agreed upon and to the commitment of the stakeholders that have participated.

Obtaining Additional Citizen Input

The first public meeting for receiving testimony should be well publicized, provide ample space for interested parties to attend (a high school auditorium or gym is a good place), and television (or other available media) should be available to let all citizens observe and hear the dialogue. Further, once the decision guidelines are clear this is a time for the school board and the superintendent to listen.

Budget reduction and budget development both should afford opportunity for citizen input in public session prior to a final decision. Usually this takes the form of testimony at a central location during a regularly scheduled board meeting. In addition to taking testimony at regular board meetings, other options may exist, and may be desirable in times of a budget crisis. For example:

1. A special board meeting, with no action items scheduled, to hear from the general public;

2. Area meetings, in large districts, outside of a regular board meeting, conducted by selected board members. In other words, individual board members can "take the hearing to the neighborhood";

3. The use of a telephone hot line to receive questions or comments from those unable to attend sessions, or to give ideas between board meetings;

4. Distribution of a synthesized version of the recommended reductions to be housed in the community libraries, each school building and other public locations; and,

5. Presentations to key community groups with opportunities for questions.

Numerous other avenues may be available for public input, depending upon the size of the community and the time available prior to a final decision. The point here is: *Aggressive efforts to inform the general public are mandatory.* In other words, it is better to make the final board approval be a celebration of completion of the task. The aforementioned meetings are not the time to dwell on the negative aspects of the budget reduction process. It is time for action. All debate should have taken place in previous board sessions.

Taking Action

When the school board completes the review process, the official action phase takes over. This is done at a regular or special board meeting, amply publicized, and with sufficient lead time for interested parties to observe. The amount of time is dependent upon the requirements in board policy or state law. Some states allow school boards until the end of the fiscal year, June 30, to determine the budget for the next year. Other states require a much earlier date for this to occur.

Regardless of the time frame for the board decision on the final district budget the decision meeting should be well publicized with information readily available to all interested parties. Several options exist for school board action depending on the circumstances. A few are noted here:

1. Adopt the package of recommended reductions in total with no revisions. (There are several instances where school boards did this and received community/staff praise for a clear, decisive action.)
2. Adopt recommended reductions by dollar levels. An example might include a basic dollar reduction amount, with additional levels to be implemented if revenues were less than expected at that time. This would allow the board, staff and community time to wait for a final decision on a total revenue loss from the state level. (One school board adopted this plan, based upon waiting for the legislature's final funding plan for schools.)
3. Adopt a given level of reductions along with a revenue generation plan. (For example, implementing an energy conservation savings plan.) This would hold in abeyance future reductions if the revenue plan did not meet expectations. It would also intensify the interest in making the revenue plan work.
4. Adopt a revised plan resulting from board deliberations. Hopefully, this would not include major revisions. For example, one school board revised the reduction list by $113,000 from a $13.5 million plan.

Usually board decisions of a policy nature are finalized only after a two or three step process that allows for additional thinking time. An example is the first reading and second reading process used by many boards. A minimum of two weeks and as long as a month between the readings are the norm. Certainly, with the magnitude of this decision, some time should be allocated.

The Aftermath

The school board's final decision may indicate to some that the immediate job is over. Not so. Several tasks must be completed as quickly and accurately as possible.

1. Employees must be informed of board action and the implications. A fact sheet summarizing board action should be distributed to all district worksites and employees the day after board action.
2. School or area meetings should be established for employees (who have questions) to attend and obtain answers. The size of the district will dictate the number of sessions and the number of locations.
3. A summarizing fact sheet should be provided to all primary stakeholders who participated in the process.
4. A special meeting should be held with the board chair and superintendent for four reasons:
   a. Report board action;
   b. Clarify any issues surrounding board action;
   c. Determine if further meetings are necessary if board action includes phased reductions.
   d. Thank the members of the staff and community for their assistance.
5. A fact sheet should be provided to each board member for use with constituents and the media.
6. A telephone hot line should be established for staff and citizen use for at least one month after board action. It may also need to be in place at the beginning of the next school year so that par-

ents can call with questions about the impact of the budget reductions.

7. The superintendent must realize the emotional impact of the final decision; he or she must continue the communication efforts into the next school year. People, employees, parents, citizens, etc., will need to discuss the changes with someone and be reassured that the plan is working. The superintendent must work to normalize the situation.

Other actions may be necessary depending on the local situation. However, normalizing the situation must be a priority for all key district and building staff. The district must begin to work with whatever budget has been approved, as the goal of educating the community's children has not changed or been removed.

Authors Note: There are no worksheets included for chapter 13. The board will be working with the package of information compiled and submitted by the superintendent. In approving the product, the board should not be in the business of creating new documents.

Reference

Blanchard, Kenneth, John P. Carols, and Alan Randolph (1996). *Empowerment Takes Under a Minute.* San Francisco, CA: Berrett-Kochler Publishers, p. 15.

Section Four

Moving On To Better Times

Chapter Fourteen

Leadership after the Financial Crisis

In the final analysis, it is all about people. (Klann 2003)

Chapter Assumptions: Three main assumptions lie at the end of the process.
1. The budget is reduced; the district must operate within the new limits. All positive suggestions for effective operation will be appreciated.
2. Think: *The budget is now final.* Negative communication accomplishes nothing. Avoid them.
3. When additional revenue becomes available budget restorations are guided by the same planning process. The principle of "last out, first in" should apply, given normal circumstances.

Chapter Objectives: The goal of the entire budget reduction process is to emphasize the "Three R's."
1. Return to Normalcy.
2. Review and Adjust.
3. Re-energize the District.

Return to Normalcy

A financial crisis brings out a myriad of emotions for employees and the community in which it occurs. Uncertainty can become the order of the day. Employees can feel threatened and community members may feel betrayed when each becomes aware of the nature of the financial crisis and what it might do to their livelihood or the hopes and dreams for their children. Leaders need to recognize those most directly impacted by the crisis may, if not led effectively, demonstrate behaviors and actions that are counterproductive to solving the crisis.

Leadership during a financial crisis has been the primary focus of this manual, but, in reality, leadership after the crisis is as important. First and foremost, the superintendent must communicate to all stakeholders that plans are in place to address another financial crisis if one should occur. The superintendent should indicate the three levels of reduction recommendations (*the most immediate, the most probable, and the worst-case scenario)* are in place as a fail-safe plan to avoid a repeat of the situation they just experienced. Further, the superintendent should emphasize that all information about school board budget decisions is readily available to all employees and community members. Finally, the superintendent should reassure all stakeholders that steps will be taken to monitor the financial situation in the immediate months and years ahead. Hopefully, the budget situation will improve and some programs

179

will be reinstated. But if the financial difficulties continue, then the process just completed can be reactivated immediately. The message should be clear: the district had a well thought out plan of work and the plan was implemented. The process would work again if needed.

Establishing avenues for employees and community stakeholders to meet with the superintendent, school board members, and senior staff to receive accurate information and ask questions is essential. Many of the strategies utilized during the crisis should be continued but for a different reason. Clearly, those strategies that proved to be the most effective should become a part of the fabric of the school district. Examples would be the superintendent's TV show, caller hot line program, the Cost Busters program, area meetings in large districts, regular meetings with bargaining unit and employee association leaders, and selected community groups. The communication strategies employed should not only enhance communication in general but help employees reconnect with the district values, priorities, and specific initiatives. All of these efforts should be designed to return the district to normal operations as quickly as possible.

Review and Adjust

A critical review of the financial crisis, the impact it had on the district, the specific issues that formed the basis for the crisis, the district's response, and each of the activities undertaken to alleviate the crisis should be evaluated as soon as possible after all board decisions are implemented. This should not be to fix blame; rather, it should be examined to determine what could be done to avoid another crisis or collect information about what was most effective in solving this present crisis. This review is best done with the help of individuals who were directly involved in planning and implementing the six-step process. The reasoning is simple: those who were involved in the process should be involved in discussing and refining the process.

An analysis of the effect of the crisis on the district should also be started as soon as possible. The findings of these activities should be communicated to all employees and community stakeholders. Further, the known causes of the crisis should be studied and the results shared with all stakeholder groups. If local or state government officials, both elected or appointed, can provide assistance with this assessment it would be beneficial. The goal is to work to avoid such crises in the future.

Finally, the findings of the district should be communicated to all local and state officials so they clearly understand the situation the district faced and the district response to the crisis. In many instances the elected or appointed officials have been busy addressing the crisis at a different level and have not internalized the impact on the local school district. Also, this provides an opportunity to review the six-step process with them and to provide them with a clear picture of how the district intends to address any additional financial crises, if the need arises. One district held a work session with local and state officials and reviewed each step of the process and how the district focused their efforts to solve the crisis. This was well received by participants and reinforced the message that the crisis was managed in an orderly, systematic manner.

Re-energize the District

Reinvigorating the school district after a financial crisis requires a targeted focus on critical leadership skills by the superintendent and the senior leadership staff. While the stakeholders may demonstrate relief that the crisis is over, experience indicates some time is required before those same stakeholders feel comfortable about getting on with their careers and lives, without the worry of when will the other shoe drop. The superintendent should emphasize to senior and building leadership that sensitivity to employee and citizen issues/concerns is of utmost importance. Further, the superintendent should assertively reconnect employees and the community with the primary goals and objectives of the districts' plans for the future. In other words, put them to work on those activities, projects, and events that will aggressively move the district forward.

People want to get back to normal when a crisis is over. Unfortunately, they might not clearly know what they should focus on to achieve this goal. The superintendent and district leadership have a responsibility to help them accomplish not only their personal goals, but also those of the school district. However, a word of caution is in order: Micromanaging is not the way to achieve these goals. The superintendent, along with other district leaders and the school board, should remember the process that was used to address the financial crisis: *collaboration.* During the crisis employees and community members were asked for their advice and counsel to find ways to solve the crisis. District and building leadership were expected to administer their responsibilities, with little direction from the district, while focusing on ways to handle the financial crisis. Reinvigorating the district must include these two beliefs: Work together to do your job, without constant supervision and micromanaging.

An example may serve to focus these beliefs. One of the authors assumed the superintendency of a large school district after a prolonged teacher strike. While an assistant superintendent of the district, that individual had the opportunity to work across the district with a variety of district and building leaders to manage the district response to the strike. A fundamental principle of district leadership during the strike was "let the building and district leadership do their job." In addition, building and district leadership met regularly to determine what was being done effectively and to obtain advice about how things could be improved.

When the strike was concluded and the author became the new superintendent, building and district leaders were brought together and asked: What have we learned? What can we do better to avoid, if possible, another strike occurring in the future? What changes should we make to ensure the most effective operation of the district?

The response was simple. "Let us do our job." Provide us with the goal and let each of us determine the best ways to achieve the goal in our work setting. Do not micromanage us as was done before the strike. The new superintendent listened carefully and subsequently, after careful planning with leadership representatives, implemented "site based management." The process resulted in a substantial increase in student achievement and both efficiency and effectiveness of the delivery of support services.

Summary

Much literature is available about how to handle a crisis. Very little of it directly focuses on addressing a financial crisis, although many of the same principles apply. The summary of needed crisis leadership components is outlined by Klann (2003). He states they are the three "C's" of crisis leadership. District leaders must show constant communication, clarity of vision and values, and caring.

Reference

Klann, Gene (2003). *Crisis Leadership, Using Military Lessons, Organizational Experiences, and the Power of Influence to Lesson the Impact of Chaos on the People You Lead.* Greensboro, NC: Center for Creative Leadership, p. 69.